The Owl in
Monument Canyon

The Owl

in Monument Canyon

and Other Stories from

Indian Country

H. Jackson Clark

Foreword by

Terry Tempest Williams

University of Utah Press

Salt Lake City

Illustrations by Mica Clark

Printed on acid-free paper.

Library of Congress Cataloging-in-Publication Data

Clark, H. Jackson, 1924–
    The owl in Monument Canyon, and other stories from Indian
country / H. Jackson Clark ; foreword by Terry Tempest Williams.
    p. cm.
    ISBN 0-87480-438-8 (cloth : acid-free paper). — ISBN
0-87480-439-6 (paper : acid-free paper)
    1. Clark, H. Jackson, 1924– . 2. Art dealers—Southwest, New—
Biography. 3. Navajo Indians—Textile industry and fabrics.
4. Pueblo Indians—Textile industry and fabrics. 5. Indians of
North America—Southwest, New—Social life and customs.
6. Southwest, New–History. 7. Southwest, New—Description and
travel. I. Title. II. Title: Owl in Monument Canyon.
E99.N3C533 1993
709'.2—dc20
[B]   93-23911

*To my grandsons, Edward Jackson Clark
and Nickolas Oliver Clark, sixth generation
Durangoans and Southwesterners.*

Contents

Foreword

Jackson Clark is a raconteur, a storyteller, a man who holds much of the history of the American Southwest in his bones. His roots are deep and secure in this region, wrapped tightly around sandstone boulders much like the great junipers with their gracious character. The open country, the slickrock canyons and mesas, the dry winds that carry the sweet smell of sage across the land— please him, inspire him, and inform his life.

Jackson Clark stands his ground in both time and place as a vital citizen of the Colorado Plateau. He is native.

I remember the day we met, vividly. The Utah Museum of Natural History was hosting its annual Indian Arts and Crafts Show with the Toh-Atin Gallery from Durango, Colorado. It was a family enterprise with Jackson at its helm, his wife Mary Jane and their two children, Jackson Clark, Jr., and Antonia. This was a celebrated gathering within our community, a time to honor the artistic traditions of Navajo weavers, Hopi, Zuni, and Navajo silversmiths, Pueblo potters, and Indian artists, in general. It was a week in May that wed culture and nature through story, the stories inherent in art.

Jackson Clark shook my hand. I was new to the museum. He asked me what I was interested in. I told him I had been spending time on the Navajo Reservation, that I was studying their oral traditions and working with some of the children in Montezuma

Creek, Utah. Immediately, his eyes flashed enthusiasm and I recognized in this tall, dignified man a deep love and respect for not only the land, but the people who inhabit the land. Navajo country was in his blood.

We walked over to the rugs. He identified each one. "This is a Storm Pattern. This is a pictorial. This is a Two Grey Hills. Ganado Red. Wide Ruins. Yei." Each rug wove a story connected to a person and a place. Louise Tsosie. Mary Begay. Mr. Yellowhair. Even the names held magic. Chinle. Monument Valley. Many Farms. I began to see not only the depth of experience behind Jackson Clark, as a contemporary trader with a strong linkage to his past, but the depth of his convictions. Here was a man genteel and sophisticated, at once, who was encouraging, supporting, and illuminating the native traditions he holds in such high esteem.

Jackson Clark is a passionate and humble man.

In the book you hold, *The Owl in Monument Canyon*, is a life well lived. It is a collection of vibrant, moving, oftentimes humorous stories gathered up in the name of desert relations. Traders. Indians. Human beings, brought together originally through commerce, in the end alter each other in the shared experiences of what it means to dwell in arid country. Anyone who has traveled in the Four Corners knows this is not an easy ride. Jackson Clark has traversed this territory of Indian and Anglo disputes with as much grace as anyone I know. His stories show us what is possible. They create a bridge between cultures. A healing.

Last spring, Jackson Clark took Mary Gesicki (former curator of education at the Utah Museum of Natural History) and me out to visit some of the Hispanic communities in northern New Mexico. With typical wit and charm and savvy, Jackson spun us in and out of stories. He introduced us to various mayordomos and artisans. He took us inside churches and outside galleries. Everything Jackson saw was of keen interest to his soul. And once again, it was the people in place that moved him.

But what I remember most about our day in the mountains is our entry into the Church of San José de Gracia. The smell of piñon smoke was strong. Bluebirds circled the old adobe in Las Trampas built in 1760. We were the guests of a villager, a friend of Jackson's. Once inside, we sat on weathered wooden pews.

Graves were beneath the floorboards. Seven across. Ten deep. I could feel their unnamed bones beneath me.

"José Raphael Aragon," Jackson whispers. "He is the artist who brings life here. You can follow his paintings throughout many churches in New Mexico." Jackson points to a red sun and moon peering out from behind the Spanish Christ. The Santos, the Stations of the Cross, the carved vigas, hold the centuries of devotion we have come to witness.

As we leave, I notice Jackson quietly leaves a generous contribution where community activities are posted and an offering jar has been placed.

Once outside, the mayordomo shakes Jackson Clark's hand.

"It is so good to see you again, Señor Clark."

We all feel that way.

                                                    Terry Tempest Williams

Preface

I planned for many years to write a book about people and places I have known in the Southwest. Planning to write and writing are two different things. I had writer's block, but didn't know what it was. During the summer of 1978, while taking a creative-writing course in California, I began a book on Navajo culture and weaving. I worked on it again during the summer of 1979, but lost interest in it, and it never got off the ground. It wasn't what I wanted to write about. I wanted to write about people: traders, weavers, medicine men, and adventurers.

Then, in 1987, I pulled up stakes in Durango and moved to Chinle where I had time to visit old friends, make new ones, and explore the reservation. In 1988 I moved to Santa Fe.

My son, Jackson II (people call him J. C.), asked me when I was going to start writing about John Wetherill, Father Liebler, Harry Goulding and many others.

I had misgivings. "Look, Jackson, if the book takes three years to write, and I think it will, I'll be sixty-seven before it's finished."

"That's true. But how old will you be if you don't write it?"

Hassell Bradley, a writer in Denver, called me one day. "Jackson, your kids, J. C. and Antonia, tell me that you want to put some of your marvelous stories down on paper and write a book. Why don't you get busy? The next time you're in Denver come in and I'll help you." That cinched it. I got down to work.

Hassell did more than help me. She prodded me, she pushed me, she encouraged me, and she believed in me. She agreed to edit each chapter and to consult with me on the entire book. Sometimes her red pencil marks infuriated me, but she'd always end with an encouraging note. "This is going to be good. Don't give up. Stick with it and you'll be proud of it."

J. C., his wife Rose, and Antonia encouraged me along the way. I sent them countless drafts, and their comments were clear, concise, and constructive.

Then I met Janet (I call her Mica). She offered to help with the book. We would spend hours discussing chapters and ideas and sorting old photos that helped to sharpen my memory. One day she came to me with a drawing of Santiago's concha belt. "I think I can do some nice illustrations if you'd just get busy and finish writing."

Chapters rolled out of the printer, and even the rewrites were enjoyable. Mica said, "See how much easier it is for you to write now as compared to a few months ago? I just love to watch you work when things are going right. You're like a pianist playing his favorite tune." Later on, after we had married, she prodded me by doing drawings even before I had finished a chapter. She anticipated what I had in mind and worked in harmony with me. She made the writing fun, and it's her book as much as mine.

I owe a great deal to Larry Kershisian, a talented writer from Denver, for his valuable advice and guidance. Larry took over from Hassell when her work load became too heavy.

I am especially grateful to Dr. Robert Delaney, former director of the Center for Southwest Studies at Fort Lewis College in Durango. Bob gave me that final push and suggested that I submit the manuscript to the University of Utah Press. He helped me pin down dates and furnished the Updyke photos of Buckskin Charley.

Joe Ben Wheat, from Boulder, went along on some of the jaunts in 1987 and '88. Always supportive, Joe would show up on a moment's notice to take a trip to a place that was new to us both. His knowledge of history, archaeology, and Navajo weaving made each day a special one.

Joan Liebler gave me valuable insights into the life and times of her late husband, Father Baxter Liebler, the Desert Priest, and their life at Bluff and Hat Rock.

Mike Goulding, in the final months of her life, shared with us stories of her years with Harry building their business in Monument Valley.

I gratefully acknowledge the stories I heard from my Navajo, Pueblo, and trader friends. Surely if there is a real story in this book it is the story of the Indians and the traders I have known since childhood. Their universal warmth, humor, and friendship made it all worthwhile.

My special thanks to my daughter Antonia, my son Jackson, and his wife Rose who stood by me with love and understanding during a critical time.

I want to thank my parents, Frederick H. and Marguerite Clark Cantrell, and my sister Tonia Bennett. We were a close-knit family. Together, many years ago, the three of us lived all the stories I tell. Dad had a goal of exploring some new place at least once a month. He said, "If you live to be a hundred you'll never be able to see all there is to see in the Southwest."

I'm not a hundred, but with two-thirds of a century come and gone, I know how right he was. This is my parents' and Tonia's story as much as it is mine.

My sincere thanks to Terry Tempest Williams for writing the lovely Foreword. Her writing has always been an inspiration to me and her support helped me over the finish line.

Without Jeff Grathwohl, my editor at the University of Utah Press, this book might not have seen the light of day.

And to those many people, living and dead, who accompanied me down this road of adventure, I say, "Thank you."

The Owl in
Monument Canyon

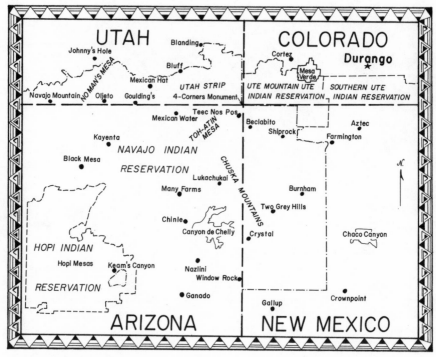

The Four Corners Region.

Introduction

I'm a Southwesterner, a native of the Four Corners area, where the states of Colorado, Utah, Arizona, and New Mexico meet at a common point. I was born in Durango, Colorado, in 1924, a fourth-generation Durangoan. At that time Durango still retained much of the frontier vitality and mentality of the Old West. Horse-drawn wagons were as numerous as automobiles. The iceman delivered ice from a wagon, and an aged milkman coaxed his ancient horse and delivery cart through the neighborhoods. Winter snows were cleared from the streets and sidewalks by a team of huge horses pulling a modified farm plow. Many homes had no electricity and some had no running water.

My Southwest is a land of stark contrasts. It is fourteen-thousand- foot peaks, lush green forests, and rushing rivers. My Southwest is the desert and the red rock mesas of Navajoland and the deep canyons of southeastern Utah. My Southwest is the small towns and isolated settlements of Anglos, Indians, and Hispanics whose mixed culture has helped define me.

Throughout my entire life I have been lucky enough to be at the right place at the right time. I was blessed with parents who loved the West and had a spirit of adventure. Many of the stories in this book took place a generation or more ago when I was a child roaming the deserts and the mountains with my parents, Fred and Marguerite Clark, and my sister, Antonia. My Dad was one of

Ute camp next to Jackson Hardware, during La Plata County Fair,
1910. Strater Hotel on left.

those fellows who never met a stranger. Because of him I became
friends with some of the legendary characters in the Southwest. In
the earlier days we knew John and Louisa Wetherill of Kayenta,
Harry and Mike Goulding at Monument Valley, and Earl Morris,
who was excavating the Fall Creek Basketmaker cave near Durango. In later years I knew Louis L'Amour and Father Baxter Liebler from Bluff, Utah. There were hundreds of other interesting
people, all with a story.

Though I could ascribe my experiences to luck, it went beyond
that. It was the result of planning, listening, observing, and remembering. My father always said that there were three kinds of people:
those who watched things happen, those who made things happen,
and those who didn't know that anything was happening. My family made things happen.

In many ways I'm a bridge, a link, between the lifetimes of the people in this book, even my own parents and grandparents, and friends in the late twentieth century.

My family loved Navajoland and the Navajo. We spent most of our weekends roaming the reservation and adjacent country. I recall watching Navajo weavers work at their looms in remote hogans off the beaten path back in the 1930s. That was when Navajo rugs sold for pitifully little money, and traders struggled to sell their rug inventory to raise money for the grocery wholesaler. Navajo weaving was poorly regarded and certainly was not the folk art it is today.

I am proud to have been a partner in the Durango Collection, a premier collection of Southwestern weaving. I am proud that together with my family we founded a business, Toh-Atin Gallery in Durango, which continues to buy and sell fine Indian art to customers all over the world. I'm proud of my son Jackson II and my daughter Antonia who now own and operate Toh-Atin Gallery. They continue our commitment to Indian weavers and artists.

Our family was always active in community affairs and in helping to make the Four Corners a better place to live. Fort Lewis College in Durango is an example of people working together to create something extraordinary. Established as an army outpost, it became a school for Indian children and finally, with a great community effort, the State of Colorado made it a degree-granting college. The modern campus sits on a mesa overlooking Durango. There are now four thousand students, including several hundred Indian students who receive a tuition-free education. I'm proud to have played a part in the growth of the college.

Navajoland attracts me like a magnet attracts iron. I have to get my reservation "fix" on a regular basis or life seems incomplete. Each time I drive to Chinle, Ganado, Gallup, or Monument Valley the memories of childhood flood back. It's all changing now, but somehow it is even better than when I was a kid. New roads are being built into previously inaccessible spots. Schools and hospitals serve the people and jobs are more plentiful.

I have seen all of these changes and met many of the men and women who brought them about. They make up the true characters in the stories I tell. Every person and every place in the book is real, although some names and places have been changed to protect my friends' privacy.

The adventure continues. I'm living in Santa Fe now with my new wife, Mica. It is an entirely different life from the one I enjoyed in Durango. But it is a fine life, a rewarding life, as we continue to expand our horizons. Every trip through the Southwest opens another chapter on a new challenge.

My Dad said I should "make things happen." I think I have.

Exploring Navajoland, 1930s

My father, Fred Clark, braced himself against the hood of our family car, scanning the horizon with his field glasses.

"Here's where we leave the beaten path and head out into the desert. I wonder how long it will take to find the Four Corners marker out there."

Dad had crammed my mother, Marguerite, my sister, Tonia, and me into the car like a bunch of gypsies in a wagon for a one-day trip to the Navajo Reservation. We did this most weeks of the year, except when the summer desert heat and the lure of a Colorado trout stream kept us home in Durango. On this particular Sunday we had driven for three hours, headed for the Four Corners, an unassuming spot in the desert where Colorado, Utah, Arizona, and New Mexico state boundaries meet at a common point.

The sleek, brown 1933 Buick four-door sedan, an unlikely car for desert travel, looked out of place on the rough reservation road. Only the large, specially built luggage trunk hinted it was a special breed. The trunk hung over the rear bumper like a strange appendage. Most folks thought it looked strange, but Dad liked it, and it did the job it was supposed to do. When the trunk was fully loaded, the front wheels of the Buick appeared to lift off the ground. It was roomy enough to hold food and water, pots and pans, sleeping bags, shovels, ropes, and other gear.

We passed through Shiprock, a trading post town on the Navajo

Fred and Marguerite Clark at Mesa Verde, 1920.

Reservation, heading west into the desert toward the distant blue outline of the Carrizo Mountains on the Arizona–New Mexico line. On our left, far south by the compass, the monolith of Shiprock, from which the town gets its name, loomed like a ghostly apparition from the desert floor.

Dad said, "See, you get a different view of Shiprock from here. It doesn't look the same, does it? We must be thirty miles from it right now. That's one big hunk of rock." Shiprock was indeed large. We had been out to it several times in the last year, the last time several weeks ago. Dad knew a Swiss mountaineer who wanted to be the first man to scale the enormous rock. We had once driven out to see his camp. Shiprock rises over sixteen hundred feet above the desert floor. The Navajos call it Tse be dahi, "The rock with wings." It is a sacred pinnacle and the source of many Navajo legends. The Navajo Nation has now banned all climbing on the rock.

We knew where the Four Corners marker was on the map, but reading the map and then finding it on the ground were two different things. Poorly defined roads or trails didn't help. We found only one sign, half-buried in the sand. It became a hit or miss, "eenie, meenie, miney, moe" kind of drive. Every fork in the road presented a new challenge. The chances of finding the monument among the cactus, rocks, and sagebrush seemed mighty slim, but I had faith in my Dad. If there was a marker out there, he'd find it. I always thought that he would have been a great explorer in the mold of the idols of the day: Martin and Osa Johnson, Frank Buck, Admiral Richard E. Byrd.

Finally, Dad said, "Let's stop and get the map out again. We aren't going to find it wandering around like we have been."

We stopped on top of a small hill, right in the middle of nowhere, and squatted down beside a flat rock that we used as a table. We oriented the map so that north on the map was pointed north on the terrain. In a few moments he had picked out landmarks on the ground and on the map and we were on our way.

We had been driving around in the desert for several hours before we finally found the Four Corners Monument, such as it was, late in the afternoon. A seldom-used trail led off of a rarely traveled road up to a small hill where we found a simple wood scaffold built over a concrete marker. A brass cap on the top of the concrete marked the spot. Dad photographed Tonia and me perched on top of the scaffold. We had driven a long way to find this place. To me it didn't seem worth the effort, but Dad was elated. "Just imagine, how few people have ever been to this exact spot. We'd never have found it without the map."

I could read a map before I could read a book. We always had maps around the house. Maps were stored on shelves, in drawers, in folders, and it was a rare day that a map for some remote place was not spread out on the dining room table. Dad would not go anywhere, even to Denver, without poring over a map before the trip.

I remember a trip to Chaco Canyon. Dad blindfolded Tonia and me when we left Aztec, New Mexico. When we reached a place near Chaco he removed the blindfolds. We piled out of the car, shielding our eyes against the bright sun. Dad said, "Now, point toward Durango." When I pointed in the wrong direction he carefully told me

Jackson and Tonia, Four Corners Monument, 1934.

how to tell north from south by the sun and lichen growing on the north side of rocks and trees.

"You pointed south. Durango is off there to the north, near the highest mountains. Here, take the compass and get yourself located and then show me on the map where we are."

This was no easy trick for a youngster, but Dad reminded me, "This is the way Navajo families teach their children to find their way home if they become lost." He continued, "They have to do it the hard way, by developing a good sense of direction. They learn how to read the sun, the shadows, and the plant life. Someday you may be lost and this could save your life. Imagine being a Cliff Dweller child, long ago, and being lost in this maze of canyons. They didn't have maps, clocks, compasses, or box lunches. They had to do it all by their wits and knowledge of nature. When you are out in the wilds always keep your eyes open. Always be aware of where you are, where you have come from, and where you are going. The easiest way to get lost is to daydream and start walking in circles." I never forgot his advice.

Jackson Hardware, 1936.

I didn't always like the weekend trips. Some were fun; others just seemed long and wearing. On this trip I was ten years old and Tonia was barely five. But we were already old hands at backcountry travel. Our parents, seldom content to stay at home for a quiet weekend, planned way ahead for these jaunts. When Sunday rolled around, or on Saturdays when Dad didn't have to work at Jackson Hardware, we took off to some new and little-known point on a map.

Dad never saw a side-road, a washed-out trail, or a mountain pass he didn't yearn to explore. He liked the new and the different. He didn't care to sit around, play cards, listen to the radio, or socialize when strange places beckoned. I always smelled adventure when planning these trips. We might as well have been off to Kenya as Kayenta. His typical comment was, "I wonder what's up that road?" Or, "That canyon looks interesting. Let's mark it on the map and plan to come back down here later in the year."

That was the pattern. Dad talked to everyone he knew who had any knowledge at all of the area we wanted to see. He carefully assembled maps, camping gear, water, ropes, tire chains, extra gasoline, and food. The Buick received meticulous service. When we drove out of Durango we were ready, really ready.

Dad didn't leave much to chance. He hadn't been in the army during World War I, but he knew how to organize and motivate without wasting time or energy. He knew how to get things done. I think it must have been his experience in bossing telephone company construction workers in the mountains of Colorado, Utah, and Idaho. He had designed and built the telephone links between such Colorado mountain towns as Silverton, Ouray, and Telluride.

Counting the 1933 Buick, we went through four cars during those reservation years. First, there was a 1929 Buick sedan, precursor to the Sherman tank. It had ample power, plenty of clearance, a big trunk, plus running-board storage boxes for all our gear. In 1932 we got the '33 Buick, which Dad later traded for a 1937 Buick Roadmaster. The Buicks were often coaxed into places I'd hate to take a modern four-wheel-drive vehicle today. After the '37 Buick came a 1941 Lincoln Zephyr sedan, a poor desert car. It had too much overhang, front and back, and rode too close to the ground to go where we wanted. But it was a good-looking car and Mother loved it.

Two instances stand out with the '33 and '37 Buicks. First, the '33 was almost new when we drove it on its first reservation trip. We had been to Gallup, Fort Defiance, and Lukachukai and were climbing out of Lukachukai toward the summit of Buffalo Pass on our way back to Shiprock. It was a wicked road with lots of rocks, steep dropoffs, and mudholes. At the top of the pass, in the middle of the magnificent ponderosa pines, we came across a group of Navajo CCC men. The Civilian Conservation Corps was founded by the Roosevelt administration during the depression to give jobless young men a chance to make a living in a semimilitary environment. We knew about camps at Durango and Mesa Verde National Park, but this one high on Buffalo Pass surprised us.

The Lukachukais are formidable mountains. Ponderosas as large as seven feet in diameter thrive on the mountain. Aspen, gamble oak, and fir trees are abundant. It is a lush oasis rimmed by dry, barren desert on the east and west. From the summit it is possible to look east to the high mountains in Colorado and west as far as Black Mountain and Monument Valley. To the north is the crimson, pink, and purple rock country of Cove Valley between the Lukachukai and the Carrizo mountains. Rich uranium deposits

1929 Buick.

1933 Buick.

were later discovered and mined during World War II. Twenty miles to the east, Shiprock, the rock itself, sailed across the desert floor, dwarfing the huge sandstone bluffs and buttes.

As we approached the CCC camp, a young Navajo man, a recruit in his newly issued olive-drab uniform, thumbed a ride. Dad said, "Yá'át'ééh," probably the only Navajo word he knew, and, "Hello. Where you headed?"

"To Red Rock to see my mother."

Dad told him to sit in the front seat. Tonia, Mother, and I crowded together in the backseat. Dad offered the man a cigarette and then pushed in the electric cigarette lighter on the dashboard. The Navajo had never seen a lighter like that. He reached into his pocket and took out a wooden, sulfur-tipped match, which he struck on the dashboard of the car. Horrified, Dad tried to stop him. The match flamed and cigarette smoke curled up from the front seat. A long, yellow mark marred the metal face of the glove box. After the shock wore off, Dad smiled and winked at Mother in the backseat. Then he showed the young Navajo how to use the lighter.

When we got home we tried to remove the sulfur mark but it was there to stay. Several years later, when we traded the car in on the '37 Buick, the mark remained.

The 1937 Buick was larger, longer, and heavier than the 1933. It was more difficult to steer around sharp corners, and it didn't have that magnificent, spacious trunk.

One Sunday we were on our first trip from Bluff, Utah, to Mexican Hat. The road, a dimly marked path over the rock mesas, wound through a series of arroyos piled with rocks and debris. After we got down into the arroyo Dad had second thoughts about the trip.

"I heard that this might be a miserable road, but I didn't think it would be this bad. Maybe we'd better find a place to turn around and go back to Bluff and see if we can find some ruins to explore."

No sooner had he said this than we came head to head with a big Dodge truck, loaded with cedar fence posts, and driven by an angry-looking, red-faced old white man, a huge fellow with a reddish gray beard and cold gray eyes. He piled out of the truck and stomped toward our car.

1937 Buick.

"What the hell are you doing down in here with that car? Do you know where you're going?" Without waiting for an answer he ordered Dad to back up and do it in a hurry.

"Just keep backing until I can get around you. This country is not the same anymore. A feller can't hardly get out of town without running into traffic. Now, just back up like I say. Back up!"

Dad was mad, Mother was mad, and I wanted Dad to use his .22 pistol and shoot the guy. Calmer heads prevailed and we backed for almost a mile before the truck could squeeze by. The huge man, looking more like a giant with each passing moment, got out of the truck, slammed the door, and stalked up to the Buick. It looked like trouble, serious trouble. Showdown gully.

He squatted alongside the driver's door and said, "I'm sorry I got so gosh-darned cross. I got a bunch of Navvys working on a fence for me and I have to get these posts to them. If you're serious about going on down that gully, you'll have some hard hills about a mile from where I met you. After that it's pretty easy going. You ought to be in Mexican Hat in about two hours." They chatted for a while. Dad poured the fellow a stiff shot of bourbon from the flask we always had in the car. They parted friends.

Not one to let a little rough road stop him, Dad forged ahead and got us to the trading post at Mexican Hat about dark. The Buick proved itself, and a one-day trip turned into a two-day adventure.

When Tonia and I tried to beg off a long trip, we heard the same story time and time again. "We are going to places that most people

1941 Lincoln Zephyr, Shiprock.

don't even know about. We will see Indians whose way of life is changing. When you grow up these things will be different. Even the roads and the towns will change. We want to see it now, like it is. Someday you'll understand."

Now I do understand; I have for a long time. I'm grateful for those days, weeks, and years when we prowled around the Indian country. I had the chance to see and meet hundreds of interesting people. Some of them like John Wetherill, Harry Goulding, and Jesse Nusbaum of Mesa Verde became legends. Some were just common people, Navajos, Utes, and traders, but all played a part in shaping my future and focusing my life.

We sometimes saw unusual events. Once we picked up a Navajo woman and baby hitchhiking to their home north of Fort Defiance. As we rounded a bend in the road we saw a hogan on fire. The woman began wailing. "Oh! they're burning the hogan! My father must have died in it and they're burning it!" We let her off and she ran toward the flaming log hogan and into her mother's arms.

On a trip to the Hopi mesas we saw a funeral procession leave a house on First Mesa and walk down the steep trail to a burial spot on the desert floor. Frequently we would just happen onto a Squaw Dance or a Yeibichai dance, or a ceremony at a Rio Grande pueblo. My folks knew how to handle themselves and we never intruded. We always had gifts for such occasions: coffee, oranges, apples, flour, and candy. We sat in on many ceremonies when I was too young to appreciate them. Few of the Indians spoke English and we spoke no native language. But we always felt welcome.

I learned to observe, to listen, and to learn and developed a life-long fascination and understanding for the Navajo, Hopi, Apache, and Pueblo people. The more I travel the Southwest, the more I find to see. There are unmapped roads, hidden settlements, and remote canyons everywhere. Adventure is where you find it.

John and Louisa Wetherill, Labor Day, 1939

It was Labor Day weekend 1939, a time my family had anticipated. The three-day weekend gave Dad a few days away from the
hardware store. We had planned since spring to go to Kayenta and
Monument Valley, places few people in Durango had visited or
even knew existed. Dad wrote to John Wetherill in Kayenta and
Harry Goulding in Monument Valley. He carefully marked a map
for the entire trip, measuring distances, locating landmarks, and es-
timating driving time.

We loaded clothes, equipment, and food into every available
space in the '37 Buick. Mother included a special box of goodies
for the Navajo families along the way. Checking the load, we found
Dad's camera had been left in the house. He went nowhere without
the bulky old Kodak that he had owned for years.

Just as we pulled away from the curb, our neighbor, Mary
McLean, called out. "Fred! Marguerite! Wait! I have news! France
and Britain declared war on Germany!" Mary, a normally reserved,
elderly Scottish lady, ran toward us screaming, "I just heard it on
the radio! Oh! Heavens! I wonder what it means for all of us?"

Only days earlier, Nazi troops had slammed into Poland in the
world's first taste of blitzkrieg. Adolf Hitler expected an easy vic-
tory and only a slap on the wrist from Britain and France. He had
taken Austria, Czechoslovakia, and the Rhineland in bloodless

Fred Clark's Kodak Model #A Special.

conquests. Now he had gone too far, too fast. The jig was up. World War II began that weekend in 1939.

I had always been keenly interested in politics, history, and current events. I felt fully informed about the events in Europe, even though I had just turned fifteen. *Time* magazine and shortwave radio broadcasts had given me a good background on Hitler and his gang.

I stood in the warm sunshine, under the clear blue sky, while my folks talked with Mary. I wondered how the war would affect my friends and me. When would America become involved? Would I have to enter the army or navy? Questions piled up in my mind. For a year my parents had coaxed me to go to New Mexico Military Institute. I hated the idea. Now they'd surely bring it up again. I knew we'd talk about it on the trip. Military school was not my idea of fun.

"That damned Roosevelt," Dad said. "If he wasn't crippled, he'd dance with joy. He wanted this all along, and now he is going to get us in it too. I wish we could get some news on the radio." We wouldn't get any news until nightfall, however, since our car radio picked up only nearby stations during the day. Low-powered KIUP in Durango, the only station between Albuquerque and Salt Lake City, faded out a few miles from town. Distant stations came in only after dark.

We drove on to Farmington, New Mexico, a sleepy farming town fifty miles south of Durango, then to Shiprock, our usual reservation jumping-off point. From there the roads were mostly rutted trails after the heavy rains of August—just as we had expected. The tree-lined streets of Durango and the green fields of the Animas River valley were far behind. We had driven into high desert country, a stark, sparsely populated land dotted with mountain ranges, red rock monoliths, and deep canyons. Several times during the day we passed isolated trading posts: Teec Nos Pos, Red Mesa, and Dinnehotso. We stopped at several posts to talk to traders and tell them what we knew about the war.

Dad knew many of the traders on the reservation through their business with Jackson Hardware. We stopped to visit one family that lived in a house behind their trading post. The trader's wife prepared lunch for us and her family. Young children played in the grassless yard. I asked, "Where do the kids go to school?" She replied, "Oh, I'll tutor them until they get into the second grade. After that the children and I will move back to Farmington. We'll see my husband only every other weekend. I hate to leave him, but we have no other choice."

I remember thinking how lonely it would be for the husband. No other white families lived within forty miles. The isolation was incredible. I looked at the landscape and thought that it would make a good location for a movie about the French Foreign Legion. Forty to fifty miles separated trading posts. The traders had no electric power, no telephone, no neighbors. Small wonder that the sound of our car brought people out of their homes and stores.

Frequently we came upon Navajos traveling on foot or horseback. We stopped to offer them fruit, cigarettes, or candy. I remember Mom gave one man a hard-boiled egg, the first one he had ever seen. He watched wide-eyed as she cracked the shell on another egg, peeled it, and took a bite. Without a word he gave his egg back to her and walked off rapidly into the desert, keeping his thoughts to himself.

My mother and father loved the Navajo. They also admired the culture, the weaving, and the land. On this trip they emphasized that the war would bring changes, big changes, to the Indians.

"Pay attention to what you see, kids! Look at that old lady," Dad said. "See how she wears her hair. Look at her skirts, her jewelry, the coin buttons sewn to her blouse. Look at the old man with the necklace, his hair tied up, his old-fashioned square hat. In a few years you won't see Navvies like him anymore. I want you to see all of this. Keep your eyes open. This is all going to change."

We passed isolated Navajo settlements with herds of sheep and goats tended by a lone woman or child. Most Navajos were shy and afraid of strangers in cars. They wouldn't come close to the car even to receive an apple or oranges. Several times we left the fruit beside the road and from a distance watched the Indians investigate cautiously but curiously.

We saw many family settlements where some children played near the hogan and others herded sheep. One time a Navajo man rushed out to yank a little girl off of the road and take her back to the family hogan. He watched suspiciously until we disappeared. Dad said he might have mistaken us for government agents coming to take the child to boarding school. He said that terrified children were often forced to leave their parents' hogans and taken to boarding schools miles away. As a rule neither parents nor children spoke English. The agents who collected the children usually spoke no Navajo. The only schools for Navajo children were boarding schools. The kids went away in the fall, sometimes returning for holidays but otherwise not seeing their families for months at a time. Youngsters were punished if they spoke Navajo; English was the only language allowed in the school. Understandably, there was deep resentment and suspicion.

My mother summed it up: "Imagine if someone drove up to our home speaking a foreign language and took you kids off with them. How would you feel? How would Daddy and I react? This mandatory schooling is wrong. Why not just let them be? They're happy out here. They don't need schooling." This was a widely held opinion in the 1930s and 40s.

I thought about it all day. I wondered what it would be like to live out here. How far away would my friends live? Would I ever go see a movie, have an ice-cream soda, or take a trip? Durango looked awfully good to me.

We drove on endlessly, it seemed, deeper into the desert. The landscape changed every few miles. One minute we were driving

"We stopped to give fruit, candy, and cigarettes to Navajos along the way."

over solid rock and the next we were fighting to keep from being bogged down in soft sand. The Carrizo Mountains faded off in the background as we got closer to the imposing features of Black Mesa. It stretched off to the southwest as far as our eyes could see.

We continued to meet Navajos along the road. The rangeland seemed to be better and not so overgrazed. Recent rains had made a green carpet of the desert. Not all the Indians we met were shy. Old men on horseback stopped to wave. Some galloped to the road to see what we had to offer. Many of the Navajo men worked seasonally on the Santa Fe railroad or in the mines of Colorado and Utah. Some spoke a little English. They knew we would be a soft touch. Near Dinnehotso Trading Post we stopped to talk to a young Navajo man riding a burro. He had gathered some desert garnets he wanted to sell. Dad gave him a few coins for a handful of garnets.

I thought that we would never get to Kayenta. The rutted track wound around sandstone mesas for miles, bouncing the Buick from rock to rock, pothole to rut, and back again. Scrape marks on the stone, or an occasional car bumper, muffler, or a broken tire

Buying garnets near Kayenta, 1939.

confirmed the existence of a road. Many times we bottomed out, and we had to back out of several deep arroyos. Detours were commonplace. It was slow going and the day grew long.

We stopped to talk to every Navajo we saw along the road. Dad was a quiet, polite, and proper gent. He always stopped the car a short distance from the person. Then he'd wait a few moments, straighten his tie, adjust his hat, and step out. His big smile and warm greeting assured the Indians that he was friendly. He was a keen observer. In a few glances he saw how the individual was dressed, noted the type of jewelry he or she wore, saw the condition of his or her teeth, and estimated his or her age. It soon became a game to see who could observe and remember more than he did.

Finally, Kayenta appeared in the distance. My family had spent many weeks exploring Navajoland but we had never met John or Louisa Wetherill. Mother recalled that my grandfather had sold John and Louisa their first coal cook range when they ranched near Mancos, Colorado.

The Wetherill Trading Post and adjoining lodgings stood as the only buildings in the vicinity. They huddled against the low hill in stark gray contrast to the green cottonwoods sheltering them from the sun. Like so many twentieth-century reservation structures, they were mostly of stone construction, indicating hard work, frugality, and utility. Horses stood tied to the hitching post in front of the store. In 1939 Navajos traveled by horseback or wagon. Ours was the only car in sight.

Wetherill was closing the store for the weekend. A few Navajos lingered buying cigarettes, coffee, flour, and other supplies. Almost all the Navajo men had their hair tied in a bun, or *chongo*, and all wore turquoise beads and sported the distinctive Navajo-style square crowned hat. Calico skirts, velveteen blouses, and turquoise jewelry adorned every woman and girl.

John Wetherill was a legend in his own time, sometimes cursed, sometimes revered, but always controversial. A small man, he appeared almost frail. He didn't look like the famed explorer of the Four Corners area. John and his brothers had discovered the cliff dwellings of the Mesa Verde. John had also organized and guided expeditions, led cattle drives, and supervised archaeological digs throughout the Four Corners. Wetherill spearheaded the first expedition to Rainbow Bridge. He is credited with the discovery of the great ruins of Betatakin and Keet Seel in what is now Navajo National Monument. Still, he reminded me of an unassuming clerk who once worked at Jackson Hardware. I was surprised at his size. Of course, he was no longer a young man. It had been fifty years since the discovery of Mesa Verde, and he was seventy years old in 1939.

John and Louisa welcomed us with genuine smiles and a friendly greeting. They had heard only rumors of the war in Europe, and we spoke of it briefly as we moved our suitcases into the sleeping rooms. I remember John Wetherill calling to me as I emerged from our room. "Your grandfather is Harry Jackson, isn't he? I knew him when he was still working at Jackson Hardware. You ever been here to Kayenta before, boy?" he asked.

"No sir. I haven't. We have been looking forward to coming down here to see you for a long time."

"Well, I tell you, this is the farthest point from the railroad in the United States. There's no place more remote than this. But I think it is all going to change. There's getting to be too many people out here. Come over here and let me show you my guest book." He thumbed back through the worn book until he found the pages he sought. Holding the book so I could see he asked, "Do you know that signature, boy? And that one on the page before?" I told him I thought one name looked like Roosevelt, but I couldn't make out the other one.

"That's right. President Theodore Roosevelt," Wetherill exclaimed. "The other one is Zane Gray. You know him? He wrote western books. Both of these men stayed here in the room you are going to sleep in tonight. They stood on these same Navajo rugs, and they ate at the same table we'll be using. We've had a bunch of famous folks through here, and we made a lot of friends."

History suddenly came alive. I stood in the very place where these famous men had stood. They had actually talked with John Wetherill where I was then talking. I found it hard to believe that Kayenta was farther from the railroad than any other place in the United States. When I asked about this, John Wetherill said, "Well, let's get a map out and you show me if I'm wrong." He wasn't. We

John and Louisa Wetherill's trading post at Oljeto, 1910.

were way out in the boondocks. Years later Louis L'Amour and I stopped briefly in Kayenta and I told Louis the story of our visit in 1939. John Wetherill was a L'Amour kind of guy. The two men would have enjoyed each other.

Wetherill was in a talkative mood, which contrasts with what I heard about him in later years. He is supposed to have been a quiet man who kept his thoughts to himself. But on that day in 1939, he talked and I listened. He told me about ranching in the Mancos Valley, exploring Mesa Verde, and trading with the Indians near Monument Valley at a place called Oljeto (Moonlight Water, sometimes spelled Oljato). I wondered about the isolation and the loneliness. John picked up on my thoughts. "We brought all our goods in by our own wagons from Mancos or Durango. We had to go get it and freight it back. That trip sometimes took more than a week. Then we had to sell it and hope we'd get paid when the Navajos brought their lambs and wool in."

The terrible flu epidemic of 1918 killed many Navajos. The Wetherills left their own sickbeds to help their friends and customers. They saved hundreds of head of Navajo livestock by herding them into corrals where they would be safe from coyotes and other predators. As the epidemic raged on, John and Louisa found entire Navajo families dead in neighboring hogans. Proudly, Wetherill told me of the two infant Navajo girls they had found beside their dead parents in a hogan. The Wetherills brought the girls home and reared them as their own children.

"You'll see. They will be at dinner tonight," he told me.

At dinner we gathered at the large table in the dining room. Louisa was busy in the kitchen for much of the meal. The two Navajo girls, now grown women, served the dinner and dined with us. I remember looking around the table and thinking, "This is a happy home." I felt love and respect coming from almost everyone.

One person, however, had a disruptive influence on the meal—a missionary named "Shine" Smith, widely known as a character, off and on the reservation. My parents knew of him. Noisy and boisterous, he took an immediate shine (which is perhaps why he had the nickname) to my ten-year-old sister, a striking, tall, dark-haired girl who looked at least fourteen. Smith couldn't take his eyes off her and continually reached across the table to touch her hand. Dad was uncomfortable, my mother furious. Later John Wetherill told my dad, "We have few white friends out here, so we put up with Shine. He really don't mean any harm."

During supper we all talked about the war. Everyone thought that America should stay out of it, but all agreed that it would only be a question of time before we were involved. People hated and feared Hitler, but they also had a deep distrust in the government, President Roosevelt, and Congress.

Dad said, "I think that damned Roosevelt wants us in this thing. It's a mistake. I didn't serve in the World War, back in 1917, but I'd be willing to go now if Jackson could avoid it."

Wetherill agreed. "We're doing all right as it is. The depression is behind us, and business is good. I hate to have things changed. Let those foreigners fight it out among themselves."

It was dark by the time we finished our meal. Dad asked me to go out to the car, parked next to the dining room, and see if I could get any news on the radio. Tonia and I went to the car, switched on the radio, and began searching the dial for strong signals. KOA in Denver was loud and clear, as was KOB in Albuquerque, and even KNX in Hollywood. Most of the band was just static. However, on KNX there was an announcement that the President would speak to the nation within a few minutes. Roosevelt was famous for his fireside chats with the American people, but this was going to be more than a chat.

I rushed back to the dining room with the news. "Roosevelt is getting ready to speak. I've got a real strong station." We all hurried outside. Curious Navajos, hearing the strange sound of the radio, came from the nearby hill where a Squaw Dance was being held. Silently, they gathered around the car. John, Louisa, and the girls brought chairs for the Navajos until there were no more left to bring. Then they passed out pillows and blankets. The people, all but hidden in the darkness, strained to listen. Roosevelt's strong melodious voice filled the night air. This was the first time many of the Navajos had heard a radio.

I sat in the car's back seat watching people gather. The Navajos, all dressed in their best outfits and adorned with their finest jewelry for the Squaw Dance, showed little emotion. I thought how far we were from a town, but really how far we were from the mainstream of the twentieth century. It was a night of contrasts.

Roosevelt reviewed the events in Europe. He spoke of his sympathies, the sympathy of the American people for the Allies, and of his sorrow for Poland. He promised that America would remain out of the conflict, but we would aid the British and French in material ways. I think the term "Lend-Lease" was coined that night. The U. S. planned to loan or lease war equipment to the Allies, and at the same time try not to get involved in fighting. It was a sobering speech.

As soon as the President concluded, Dad turned the radio off. Wetherill, deep in thought, frowned and suddenly climbed up on the hood of the Buick. Tonia and I slid out of the backseat and squatted near the front wheels. Standing as straight and tall as he could, Wetherill spoke in Navajo for ten minutes or more. Not an eye shifted.

When he finished speaking and had said good night to all the Navajos, Dad asked him what he had told them.

"I told them that a great war had started on the other side of an ocean they had never seen, among people they didn't know, over a quarrel they would not understand. I told them that from this night on, their lives, and the lives of all of us, would never be the same. I told them that even I didn't understand what was happening and why it was happening, but that things were going to be different. I told them that before this war is over the United States will be involved. Navajo boys will have to join the army or the navy and they will fight and die in other countries. I told them that everything will change. They have to expect it. We shall never be the same.

"I just wonder how this will all turn out. When I think of some of these boys going off to war I get sick to my stomach. How will they manage in the army? How many will come home again?"

How true Wetherill's words were. Navajo boys were destined to fight and die in battles all over the world. Many would play important roles; the most notable were the Navajo Code Talkers, a group assembled in the Pacific Theater to speak a coded Navajo in radio messages. Since the Japanese couldn't understand Navajo, much less the complicated code, they were completely baffled. The Code Talkers played a vital role in the Pacific War. Navajo women worked in war production plants, disrupting family life. Mothers had no time to teach young daughters how to weave.

We all helped move the furniture back into the lodge and then walked in a group to the Squaw Dance site. Fires burned brightly around the field, and we saw the Navajo women in their colorful dresses.

Squaw dance ceremonies are also known as the "Enemy Way." They are great summer occasions originally intended for healing, but mostly for fun and enjoyment now. Mothers scan the crowd for a likely mate for a daughter. Young women ask men to dance. To escape the clutches of a female the men must pay money, or, as is sometimes the case, promise marriage.

Shine Smith pestered Tonia, and Mother fumed until we left about midnight. Smith annoyed her, but there was little she could do except stand close.

The next morning, after a good night's sleep and a big breakfast, we loaded our bags into the Buick, said goodbye to the Wetherills, and drove north toward Monument Valley.

When we stopped to view the Mittens of Monument Valley Mom said how much she had liked Louisa Wetherill. We all agreed. Louisa had been warm and gracious to us as well as the Navajos who gathered around the car radio. She said, "One Navajo woman called her by a Navajo name, a funny name. I wonder what it was."

Years later I read the book *Traders to the Navajo* co-authored by Frances Gillmor and Louisa Wetherill. It is the story of the John Wetherills and their life among the Dine', or the People, as the Navajo call themselves. The People named her Asthon Sosi, Slim Woman. Her friendship with the Navajo people was one of extraordinary warmth and sincerity. This unassuming woman had been on many of the explorations into remote country; she had lectured at major universities and had written several papers on the Navajo and their religion. We had met her, but we hadn't yet absorbed the depth of her spirit.

Dad died in 1946, a month after I returned from the army. I didn't go back to Navajoland until 1947. By that time, the Wetherill Trading Post and Lodge was closed and boarded up. John and Louisa had died during the war. I remember standing outside the deserted buildings thinking back to that remarkable evening eight years before. John Wetherill's words echoed in my mind. "Nothing will ever be the same again."

Kayenta, now a bustling hub of commerce and tourism in Navajoland, boasts a supermarket, two fine motels, schools, and hospitals. The old Wetherill store is gone, but a motel named for the Wetherills stands on a hill overlooking the site of the old store. Good roads lead north and south from the town. Few traces remain to tell us of two outstanding people, John and Louisa, and the mark they made on the people and places of Navajoland.

Mike and Harry Goulding's Monument Valley

Harry Goulding rode his horse into remote Monument Valley in the early 1920s. He was working as a livestock buyer for the Ly-brook Ranch located south of Farmington. Harry's job was to search for and buy the ewes and bucks of the old Navajo sheep, the rare Churro breed with long silky wool and the distinctive four horns that sometimes curl down into the face of the animal. The breed, originally introduced into the Southwest by the Spanish, had been almost wiped out by cross-breeding with Merino sheep since the days of Bosque Redondo and the Long Walk.

But in that little-known area of the Four Corners, he found more than Churro sheep. He found a place of beauty and isolation be-yond his wildest dreams and he vowed to claim part of it for him-self and his bride Leona, whom he called Mike.

Goulding, a man of unusual vision and ambition, saw opportu-nities others failed to grasp. He and Mike Knee were married in 1923, and the following year they moved everything they had to Monument Valley. Working together, Mike and Harry built and ran Goulding's Trading Post, but they wanted more than just a trading post. They wanted the world to come, to see, and to share their valley with them.

Located in the redrock country of the Navajo Reservation on the Utah–Arizona state line, Monument Valley sits in a landscape of breathtaking wonder. Few works of man mar the landscape. It is a place of stark natural beauty. The entire valley occupies only a small portion of the vast Four Corners region. You can fly over it in a few minutes, but on the ground it is overpowering. The immensity of the monuments, the emptiness of the space, and the silence overwhelm the senses. It is a place that transforms itself day by day, hour by hour, season after season. The light changes and shadows shift. Colors seem to be under the control of a master art director who switches from reds to purples, yellows to tans, greens to blues with the wave of a baton. One can spend a day just watching.

Harry predicted, with the assurance of a prophet, that one day Monument Valley's scenery would become world famous. He believed that tourists would come to marvel at the dramatic views, soak up the quiet, and learn about the Navajos. Harry and Mike worked to be ready for them.

The Gouldings' dream turned out to be a long and sometimes discouraging struggle. But now Monument Valley is a world-class tourist mecca. Travelers come from everywhere to learn about the Navajo and the ancient Anasazi. A babble of European and Asian languages mingles with the soft, melodious sounds of Navajo. At times it seems overrun by people. Yet, as the crowds disperse into the desert in tour buses and private cars, the land seems almost as empty as it was fifty years ago. The vastness of the place envelops the hordes in a blanket of solitude.

Seen on TV, in the movies, and print media, the gigantic buttes and mesas are almost a cliché to most Americans, even if they haven't the faintest idea where the place is. Advertisers have found that Valley backdrops enable them to associate rugged adventure, beauty, and solitude with their products, flocking there with models, props, camera crews, and make-up artists. Recent issues of popular magazines carry ads for cosmetics, automobiles, and a variety of food products, all filmed on location in Monument Valley. Even visitors to England in the summer of 1990 were besieged by a Guinness Ale campaign featuring the now familiar rock formations. On American TV, British Land Rovers perch precariously on a cliff's edge not far from Goulding's Lodge. Meanwhile stagecoaches race across the desert beneath the looming monuments in *Back to the Future, III.*

Monument Valley is everywhere, but it is still nowhere. A never-

Churro sheep. (Courtesy Utah State University)

never place that will knock your eyes out. But for most people it seems unreal. They have to see it in person, on the ground, to know that, yes, it is real. Invariably visitors are overwhelmed by its magnitude.

I first met Harry and Mike Goulding on a weekend trip to the reservation in 1934. I remember Harry as a tall, rather handsome fellow, with a broad, lopsided smile. He reminded me of Gary Cooper. His eyes had the squint that comes from being in the bright sunlight too long without sunglasses. My father was tall, over six feet, and Harry towered over him. A rumpled straw hat and cowboy boots added to his height. I remember him as a man who never hurried. He was calm as a priest, but, as I learned through the years, as determined as General Schwarzkopf.

That first trip seemed incredibly long. At times I walked ahead of the car removing rocks from the ill-defined road. We got to Goulding's late in the afternoon on a hot summer day. We had been in Colorado, New Mexico, Arizona, and finally Utah since morning, having driven over ten hours and two hundred fifty miles in an enormous semicircle. I was tired of riding, tired of walking, just plain tired, and Goulding's looked like heaven on earth.

Harry expected us and greeted us warmly. Dad had written several weeks before to say that we were coming, and I felt the Gouldings were glad to have visitors from the outside. They rarely had guests in those days. Harry had grown up in Durango and Aztec, New Mexico, and was no stranger to my folks.

Mike was busy preparing dinner for us in their living quarters over the trading post. She was an exceptionally attractive woman with a soft, quiet energy about her. She fixed me a glass of cold lemonade and I went out on the porch. It felt good to sit and relax admiring the desert sunset.

Harry pointed out the various landmarks and talked about the country. His stories fascinated me. He told of gold miners, Navajo raiding parties, outlaws, and Kit Carson. I listened to every word as the yarns unwound in an endless stream. Surely, I thought, he was the best storyteller I had ever heard. I could imagine myself riding over this rugged landscape at the head of a posse tracking down outlaws and renegade Indians, or maybe on army patrol duty relieving a besieged outpost.

Harry looked at me and said, "When you drove in here you saw those two big buttes, the ones that look like two hands? They're called the Mittens because they look like hands wearing mittens. That butte over on the left is called Brigham's Tomb. On the right, behind this mesa, are Merrick and Mitchell Buttes, named after two white miners who got themselves killed trying to get away with some Navajo gold."

Harry pointed toward the north. "Way off over there you can see the Henry Mountains north of the San Juan River near Hanksville, Utah. That's wild country up in there, but it's *all* wild country, most of it unexplored by white men. There's nothing like it anywhere.

"To the west of us is a great big open valley. It's called Oljeto, and that's where John Wetherill had a trading post in the early days. You've heard of John Wetherill? He and his brothers discovered the cliff dwellings in Mesa Verde while rounding up stray cattle in the canyons. John and his wife still have a store at Kayenta. Old John knows this country like the back of his hand.

"You can't see it from here, but there's a big mesa west of Oljeto called Hoskinini Mesa. Hoskinini was the leader of the Navajo clans around here. He led a band of Navajos into that rugged area

Jackson and Mitten, Monument Valley, 1934.

El Capitan (Agathla Peak) on the road to Monument Valley, 1948.

to escape Kit Carson in 1863. His band was one of the few that were never captured by the American soldiers." My ears pricked up. I'd never heard about Kit Carson's infamous campaign against the Navajo in the 1860s. Carson, a folk hero to kids my age, apparently had a dark side too. I listened intently as Harry told how the Navajos were starved into surrender in Canyon de Chelly, then marched through ice and snow to Fort Sumner, a prison camp in eastern New Mexico. There they lived in deplorable conditions for four years before being freed to return to their homeland.

The trip to Goulding's did more to stimulate my interest in history, particularly of the Southwest, than any other episode in my early life. I took in all of Harry's stories. He knew I was fascinated, and he poured it on. Harry and Louis L'Amour would have had much to share, but they never had a chance to meet.

That night we slept in a small stone cabin behind the trading post, in the same building that I occupied on subsequent trips.

People who knew Harry during his early days in Aztec and

Goulding's Lodge, 1948.

Goulding's original trading post and residence. Now houses the museum.

Durango remember him as a tall, slender cowboy, who seemed more like an adventurer. He had more on his mind than cows, sheep, and horses. He had his eye on the open spaces of Navajo-land. My Dad was like him in many ways. Neither of them could spot an unknown trail without hankering to explore it.

At breakfast the following morning Harry told us, "I knew that this place was where I wanted to spend my life. Once I had seen this valley I couldn't get it out of my mind. The vastness, the isolation, the Indians, all appealed to me. The beauty of the place haunted me, and I knew this was to be home."

The Gouldings homesteaded a section of Utah school land at the edge of Monument Valley and then set about developing a water supply and building a trading post complete with living quarters. Mike and Harry lived in a tent for two years while the building was under construction. All the stone for the building had to be quarried and cut to size.

We saw the Gouldings frequently during the years following our first visit. Harry seemed to come to Durango more and more often, and we made several trips each year to Monument Valley, Bluff, and Mexican Hat. On one three-day trip to Goulding's, Harry said John Ford, the famous movie director, would film the movie *Stagecoach* the following summer in the valley.

"They plan to bring in a crew of Hollywood people. Ford has this young actor, John Wayne, he thinks will become a star. We'll have everything ready for them," Harry said. His eyes gleamed with triumph. He had gone to Hollywood to promote the Valley as a film location. It was a long shot, but one that hit home. "I just thought that if I could get some Hollywood big shots to look at my photos, I'd be able to convince them to make a movie here."

Mike said they made the trip to California in the "country way." They just loaded up and headed out with no advance letters, no reservations, and little money. John Ford was the Hollywood big shot Goulding set out to see. Harry expected to be greeted with open arms and a big movie deal, but it didn't work out that way. Ford was not interested. I'm sure he regarded the Gouldings as nuisances and refused to see them.

Harry didn't give up. Every morning he appeared in Ford's waiting room at the studio, greeted the receptionist with a big smile, and sat down to wait. In the evening he was asked to leave. Finally, after several days, Ford agreed to see him. Mike said he probably did it just to get rid of them. When Ford saw Harry's photos of the valley he got interested. In fact they amazed him. No comparable scenery existed anywhere else in America, so Ford agreed to take a look for himself.

That first meeting led to a lifelong friendship between the two men. Ford filmed *Stagecoach* and later returned to the Valley to work on *She Wore a Yellow Ribbon*, *My Darling Clementine*, *Fort Apache*, and several others. Major Hollywood studios followed Ford's lead. Goulding's became a Navajo Hollywood.

Harry Goulding had an easygoing manner, but he could be hard and tough. I admired him because he never seemed to lose his cool; his disarming smile masked the inner determination that drove him. He hadn't built his outpost in the desert by being a pushover.

Monument Valley from Goulding's, 1948.

The movie contracts proved profitable for him and for the many Navajos who worked at all sorts of movie-related jobs. In some films several hundred Navajos signed up as riders in cowboy-and-Indian scenes. Navajos filled all sorts of off-camera jobs. Harry always insisted Navajos be given first employment rights. They were reliable, eager to work, and they trusted Goulding. He had always met them more than halfway in their dealings, and they respected him.

During the filming of John Ford's *My Darling Clementine* in the 1950s, a group of Hollywood labor organizers barged onto the set. Harry likened them to a bunch of thugs. They demanded the Navajos join the union or be fired. Mike said that Kanab, Utah, had enjoyed a near monopoly on the movie business and didn't want competition from Monument Valley and Goulding's. In her opinion the Kanab people tipped off the organizers about the nonunion Navajo labor.

"We're going to bring our own union people from Hollywood,"

the head organizer said. "This is going to be a union job, or there won't be any movie." Harry listened and suggested to Ford that they ask the organizers to leave and come back the next day, " . . . so we can talk things over."

After the labor organizers left, Harry quickly spread the word among the Indians that some white men wanted to take their jobs.

Early the following morning the organizers returned full of confidence. Goulding and Ford were waiting in an open area surrounded by rolling hills, a scene that couldn't have been more appropriate to a John Ford western. The wind whistled softly through the sagebrush and yucca. There was not a Navajo in sight. It was showdown time, but this was Goulding's territory and he had a plan.

"Are you ready to play ball our way?" the union spokesman asked. Harry and Ford didn't answer. They stared holes through the men. After several moments of tension-filled, stomach-churning silence, Harry raised his arm over his head and waved it in a "gather round boys," cavalry signal. Suddenly, several hundred armed and mounted Navajos, a few wearing war paint, rode into view and slowly closed a circle around the white men.

Harry spoke in his soft, determined voice, "These Navajos are our friends. They heard that you were here to take away their jobs. They don't like it. I suggest that you get back in your car and drive out of here quickly and quietly while I try to keep them under control. Somebody's going to get hurt if you keep hanging around here. Just leave. Now!"

No other words were needed. The organizers left like beaten dogs, never to be seen again. Filming continued, and everyone enjoyed a good laugh.

The Gouldings built more than a business in Monument Valley; they built a community out of the scattered bands of Navajos who lived nearby. The trading post became the unofficial meeting place where friends gathered to talk business and exchange news. Harry ran the business but Mike ran the trading post. I can remember her standing behind the counter dealing with the Navajos, buying rugs, and selling groceries. She loved every minute. She told me that she cried the day she left it for good.

Navajo riders costumed as Arabian desert tribesmen for the filming of
The Desert Song, *starring Dennis Morgan, 1940.*

Many times Mike and Harry had to take sick and injured Navajos
to the nearest hospital, in Shiprock. In 1949 Mike drove a critical-
ly injured Navajo youngster to the hospital. The child died before
they reached their destination. Shiprock was still a bone-jarring,
five-hour drive on roads little improved from the 1930s. Harry
said, "There are more hospitals for dogs and cats in Los Angeles
than there are out here on the reservation for a hundred thousand
Navajos. I'm going to do something about it."

The next year Mike and Harry granted a ninety-nine-year lease to
the Seventh Day Adventist Church to build a hospital for the Navajos.
This hospital still serves a vast area and a growing population.

Mike told me recently, "What goes around comes around. I'd
have died if the hospital hadn't been there. Dr. Nicholas Ashton
saved my life. He's been there for many years and he works miracles." The excellent care at the Adventist Hospital and the skill of
the staff pulled her through a serious illness in 1991 and again in
the fall of 1992.

Through the years Harry and Mike kept their eyes on the long-

Navajo couple meeting tourists, Monument Valley, 1948.

term benefits of the tourist business. Goulding expected a flood of visitors after the *Stagecoach* release, but few came and it seemed that Harry and Mike were on the road much of the time, singing the praises of their valley.

I recall that on our Labor Day trip in 1939, after we had spent time with the Wetherills of Kayenta, we stopped at Goulding's. Mike's brother, Maurice, whom we had never met, was there by himself. Maurice was delighted to have company. He too was the type who never met a stranger. "Harry and Mike are off to Phoenix talking to some tour people about bringing tourists in here. Harry has the idea that thousands of people will come here if they ever get to see what we have."

Before Maurice cooked dinner he asked us to take a ride with him down into the valley. We climbed into a modified 1935 Dodge sedan custom fitted with huge airplane tires. The oversized tires allowed the car to travel easily over the sand-dunes, in and out of arroyos, and up steep grades. We left the lodge just before sunset. The light was beautiful, and the monuments in the valley loomed all around us. The setting sun struck huge rock formations and changed the color from red to crimson. A coyote crossed the road and rabbits scurried by. We didn't see another human being. I loved the ride, not just for the scenery; the car amazed me. It was a marvel. We traveled miles into the valley, over rocks, up steep hills, floating over the largest dunes.

Maurice was an interesting fellow, much like Harry. He was an Indian trader and tourist guide par excellence, fluent in Navajo, articulate in English, and incredibly patient with everyone. In all the years I knew him, I rarely saw him flustered or upset with anyone. Still, he was bitterly disappointed when Harry and Mike gave their whole outfit, store, lodge, filling station, and tour business, to Knox College. One part of the deal was a promise of Navajo scholarships at the college. Harry and Mike felt strongly about providing educational opportunities for the Indians. I think the promise of scholarships clinched the Gouldings' gift to the college.

Maurice managed Goulding's after Knox College took over. Things changed rapidly. The college insisted on setting up tight standards, something not easily accepted by Maurice and the Navajos. "I'll tell you, Jackson," Maurice explained, "These college

Monument Valley, 1939.

people are hell to work for. I have to account for every penny. How can I tell some college fellow in Illinois, who's never been out here and doesn't know anything about the Navajo, that I paid Willie Yazzie, that Indian over there, a silver bracelet for digging a ditch? They just don't understand. They want his Social Security number and want me to withhold taxes. If I told Willie he'd not get the bracelet, he'd never do anything for me again. It's just not the same."

It never was the same. Maurice ran the outfit for ten years before resigning to manage the trading post at Red Lake near Tuba City. Finally, in 1981 Knox College sold it to the La Font family, who also own the Canyon de Chelly Motel at Chinle. Mike says that as far as she knows only one scholarship ever materialized. The Navajos just didn't want to go to Illinois for school.

The new owners continued to expand Goulding's. It became a first-class resort, with swimming pool, a comfortable dining area, and expanded accommodations. A KOA campground is close to the hospital. The school district has built a handsome new high school with a grass football field. Monument Valley looks pretty civilized now, compared to the early days.

After leaving the valley Mike and Harry bought a place in Page

Mike Goulding and Jackson Clark, Monument Valley, 1992. "Jackson, I knew you before I knew John Wayne."

where they could be near newly complete Lake Powell. Harry wanted to have a boat on the lake as the water rose behind the dam. He said, "I think if we do it right we can float back into some of those canyons that white men have never seen. We will be the observers as those remote ruins are covered up forever." Mike said that they followed Harry's plan and even found the hidden cove where explorer John Wesley Powell and his men scratched their names and the date on the canyon wall. Harry must have loved it.

Harry died in 1981 and Mike lived in Sun City or Lake Havasu City during the winter and in a large mobile home near the lodge the rest of the year. The mobile home was a gift from the La Fonts.

In June of 1992 my wife, Mica, and I visited with Mike Goulding in her home in Monument Valley. She told me, "I've known you and your family since you were just a little tiny kid. I knew you before I knew John Wayne or John Ford!"

Mica asked Mike if she and Harry ever thought that Goulding's would be as large as it is now. She replied, "Yes, of course. We knew it would. We never doubted it for a minute."

When I asked her what had been the best part of living in Monument Valley she said, "It's been my life here with Harry, working with the Navajos and meeting people from all over. And of course the view of Monument Valley from here. Look how blessed I am. You can't beat a view like that."

In 1989, the La Fonts dedicated a "Movie Museum" in the original trading post building. The building itself looks just as it did back on my first trip to Goulding's. I browsed through the museum and marveled at the changes. Harry's dream of fame for Monument Valley certainly came true. I wonder if many people actually associate the real Monument Valley with the commercials they see on TV. But they know that wherever it is it's the Real West. It's that elusive place, with plenty of room, where the air is clean, the sky blue, the rocks red.

That June in 1992 I sat on the open deck in a new block of rooms at Goulding's and looked toward the Valley. The sun had set. A purple light enveloped monuments as daylight faded and darkness came. I watched a distant, almost constant stream of headlights wend its way through the desert dusk on the black ribbon of highway that had replaced the dusty trail of yesterday.

I miss the old Goulding's, though perhaps I yearn too much for the old days. I liked the quiet, family atmosphere at the dinner table, Harry's tales, Mike's smile, and Maurice's nightly slide show. But, all in all, the "new" Goulding's is better than the old. Most local Navajos have jobs, one of the Gouldings' dreams. Tourists travel from around the globe to absorb the sights and sounds of this place. They come and they go, maybe not quite sure of what they have seen.

Nevertheless, visitors still can be alone in this isolated little corner of the Southwest. High on some overlook, or deep in a canyon they can experience real solitude, the kind that enraptured the Gouldings and captivated them. Harry and Mike built their dreamplace.

The tradition continues. I think Harry must be proud looking down on all of us and smiling. I would say to him, "This is a job well done, friend Harry, a job well done."

Mike smiled when I read this last paragraph to her.

"Do you really think that he knows about all this? I think about it a lot, but I don't know. I guess I'll just have to wait and see for myself."

Mike died of cancer on Thanksgiving Day, November 26, 1992, in her home in Monument Valley. I had talked to her earlier in the month and she had urged, "Come see me in Havasu City this winter."

Ancient Cities, 1930s

My dad and I walked single file through the sagebrush and scrub juniper trees until we came to the canyon rim. One moment we couldn't see the canyon for the underbrush, and the next instant we were on the edge of a three- or four-hundred-foot vertical cliff. I moved close to him and brushed against his leg. Heights scared me. I felt as though some unseen hand was about to reach up from the canyon to drag me over the side.

Dad touched my shoulder reassuringly. "It's okay. You'll just have to learn to trust your senses and your footing. Plant your feet solidly on the rock, and don't lean too far over. You're not going to fall and we are not going to do anything dangerous."

Before we had left home that morning my mother had warned me, "Now, you know how Dad is. He'll want to climb the cliffs and get down in that canyon. I worry that you might fall. Watch out for rattlesnakes, too." Mother was a worrier, especially if she wasn't leading the group. If she'd been along on this day she'd have urged me on. I'd heard her encourage me many times. "Come on. You can do it."

I was eleven years old on this bright Sunday morning in the fall of 1935. The two of us were out on the Mountain Ute Indian Reservation about twenty miles south of Mesa Verde National Park. We had crossed into the reservation through a gate in the barbed wire fence that separated Indian land from private land and hadn't seen a single car or human being since. It was always like this. No-body ever went to this remote area. It seemed like we had the whole place to ourselves. I could almost feel the silence it was so calm. Dead calm.

Dad and I stood and talked for a few moments. He said, "I think it is so strange that most people in Durango don't even know about this canyon country. If you tell your friends about it, don't let on where it is. Let's keep it as our secret." I agreed. It was nice to have a secret place, and both of us wanted to keep it that way.

The lead gray peaks of the La Plata Mountains stood out like sentries silhouetted against the blue sky. They dominated the land-scape far to the north of us. We could see tinges of autumn gold on the aspen trees high on the mountains. An early snowstorm had dusted the peaks with a sprinkling of white powder like sugar on a cake. The weather was warm and I wore only a long-sleeved cotton shirt. Dad wore a hat, gray gabardine slacks, a jacket with big, baggy pockets, a Pendleton shirt, and necktie.

He always wore a tie, even when he worked in the yard at home. He was a very proper Dude, a gentleman, a city man who under-stood the outdoors, equally at ease in a fancy restaurant or the wil-derness. I don't think I appreciated his versatility until it was too late and he was gone.

We perched on a slab of sandstone. Dad used his binoculars to scan the canyon wall on the north side of the canyon. It must have been more than a half mile from where we were to the north rim. He looked up and down the canyon for several minutes and then handed them to me. "Here, take the field glasses. Now, look over there. Do you see those two good-sized ruins high in the cliff, right under the La Platas? It looks like there are ten to fifteen windows in the one on the left, and a few more in the ruin on the right. Do you see them?"

I spotted the ruins in the glasses. They loomed large and myste-rious against the backdrop of the cliff, an ancient city hanging on a steep wall as though it had been pasted there.

"How did the Cliff Dwellers get up there? I don't see any trails, do you?" Dad took the glasses from me and looked toward the ruins.

"I think that the trail, handholds and all, has broken off and fallen into the canyon. You can see the big trees down there in the bottom. There's a spring there. That was probably their water supply. Let's get the map out and see if we can locate the ruins on the map."

Dad always thought that we might be able to spot a certain large ruin, but as on previous days we hadn't found it. A cattle rancher had told him that in the head of Johnson, Weber, or Mancos canyon there was a huge ruin not shown on the map. There are always rumors of "lost cities," but we never found one.

We walked away from the canyon rim and decided to explore a small canyon branch that lay a short distance to the west. The little canyon came to a distinct V, and a large stand of evergreen trees grew alongside the cliff. Dad stopped and looked down into the canyon, then he said, almost in a whisper, "Look! Down there! There's a pretty little ruin almost hidden in the trees."

Sure enough, there it was, a ruin with about ten doors or windows facing southwest, perched on a ledge in this canyon. Dad was excited. "Gosh, we have been by here several times and I didn't see it until now."

We decided we'd try to get a closer look and after a while found a precarious trail down the watercourse at the head of the small canyon. We scrambled over the rocks, slid down the talus, and made our way to the base of the cliff directly below the ruin. Then it was at least twenty feet above us. We looked for handholds or some means of access, but found none. A slender dead spruce tree leaned against the canyon wall near the ruin.

Dad looked at me and asked, "Do you think you could shinny up that dead tree and get in the ruin? I'll make sure it won't slip." Mother's words came ringing back in my ears, "You know how your Dad is. . . . "

"Yeah, I can do it, if you watch me."

"I'll watch you. Just take your time. Here, use my gloves, and I'll steady the tree." Actually, I wasn't at all sure, but after a few deep breaths I started up. It was surprisingly easy. The tree was solid, the stubs of branches provided handholds and footholds. In a few minutes I stood on the ledge next to the ruin. But when I looked down I got queasy. It was a long, long way down.

Dad cupped his hands around his mouth and shouted, "You're doing fine. Take your time and get a firm footing. You're probably the first human being to go in that ruin in five hundred years." I edged my way around the ledge. I tried to stand but I felt safer crawling on my hands and knees. I poked my head into a room. It was dark as a coal mine. I couldn't see a thing. The entire ruin was still in the morning shadow.

I called down to Dad, "It's dark in there. We should have brought a flashlight."

"Well, I just happen to have my little penlight." I might have known. He was always prepared.

"I've got a ball of string in my camera bag," he shouted. "I'll tie it onto a rock and toss it up to you. Then I'll tie the penlight to it and you can pull it up." A perfect solution.

In a few minutes I had the penlight and crawled back toward the dark, deserted room. It was spooky. I hoped that I would not look into the leering face of a skeleton, or find a lurking wild animal.

"What do you see? Are there any pots or baskets in there?"

I looked around and saw only a few Anasazi corn cobs and rat droppings.

"The room's empty, and it doesn't look like anyone has been here before."

He was thrilled. "How does it feel being the first person in that room for hundreds of years?" Before I had a chance to answer, the tiny beam from my penlight hit a mark on the back wall of the cave.

"It feels good, but I'm not the first person to be here. There's a smoked marking on the back wall, like someone had a torch. It's hard to read, but I think it says, 'J. W. N. Y. Oct 1910.' " Someone had been there twenty-five years before.

I looked in all the other rooms, maybe five or six in number, and then climbed down the tree. We had a good laugh about the whole episode. Dad said, "It's getting harder and harder to be the first person anywhere. But at least you are one of the first. I wonder who J.W. was and if N.Y. means New York. J.W. may be John Wetherill. He and his family explored most of these canyons after they discovered the ruins in Mesa Verde. I'd like to know." I don't know any more now than I did then, nor have I been back to what we named "J.W. House."

Anasazi ruins fascinated my father. He loved to spot "mounds"

Pueblo Bonito, 1936, before Threatening Rock demolished the section on the left.

that disclosed where surface structures had been. Quite often as we drove or hiked through the desert country, we'd find a site that could be confirmed by pottery shards. We never missed an opportunity to visit a new "discovery" and learn as much as we could.

Jesse Nusbaum, who was superintendent of Mesa Verde National Park for two tours of duty during the 1930s, was a special friend of my parents. We spent many wonderful days exploring hidden canyons in the Park. After he was transferred to Santa Fe we visited him many times. I'm sure that Nusbaum sparked Dad's interest in Chaco Canyon, particularly the magnificent Pueblo Bonito and some of the lesser ruins that Nusbaum felt had great ceremonial significance.

He also told us to be sure to see the large slab of rock that had detached from the cliff behind Pueblo Bonito. Centuries before white men first saw Chaco Canyon, the inhabitants of the Pueblo had attempted to shore up the one-hundred-thousand-ton rock that threatened to smash the pueblo. It was called Threatening Rock. Throughout Navajoland Pueblo Bonito was known as Tse-biya hani

Threatening Rock, ca. 1925.

ahi, Place of the Braced-Up Cliff. The National Park Service did what little they could to stabilize the monstrous rock by attaching cables to the rock and anchoring them into the cliff at the top. I suppose the theory was that if it slid away from the bottom it would do much less damage than if it toppled over.

All efforts to stabilize Threatening Rock ended on the afternoon of January 22, 1941, when it buckled and fell, crushing a portion of lovely Pueblo Bonito to smithereens.

A group of Navajos who were working on ruin stabilization

Balcony House, Mesa Verde, 1930s.

Harry and Louisa Jackson at Sun Temple, Mesa Verde, 1930s.

witnessed the event. According to accounts, many feared that the
end of the world was near because the rock had fallen. Sacred corn
pollen and turquoise were scattered in a semicircle around Pueblo
Bonito in an attempt to placate the Great Spirit who had allowed
Tse-biya hani ahi to fall. The collapse of Threatening Rock also had

a profound effect on my father, enough that he sent me a Western Union telegram in care of New Mexico Military Institute, where I was in school. The event was well covered in the newspapers, but he didn't want me to miss hearing about it.

Dad knew most of the Park Service people, who often told him about large, unexcavated ruins. Many of the traders on the reservation shared his enthusiasm. We often stopped at reservation stores to get directions to some remote canyon. We always carried a shovel in the trunk of the car to dig ourselves out of an arroyo or mudhole. One day I suggested that we dig for pottery in a large surface ruin near Mancos Canyon.

"I don't mind searching for ruins," Dad replied, "and it's okay to pick up pieces of broken pottery and to look for arrowheads, but I don't want to dig. I don't know anything about it. If we dig down into a pot we'd break it. Let's leave that type of thing to the archaeologists. If we found a pot, what would we do with it?"

Today there is a great public outcry against pothunters in the Southwest. Many priceless prehistoric pieces have been found and carried off to be sold for astronomical prices. It is a major threat to many archaeological sites. I'm proud of my father, who recognized his lack of knowledge and refused to dig, way back in the 1930s.

Buckskin Charley's Last Ride

When Buckskin Charley, Chief of the Ute Nation, died on 9 May 1936 at the age of ninety-six, I was deeply moved. He was more than an Indian chief—he was a folk hero to young and old alike. He was always spoken of as a "good Indian," one who had led his tribe along the path of peace and progress and onto a reservation.

I had stopped by my grandfather's house late in the afternoon on the day Buckskin Charley died. The evening *Durango Herald-Democrat* had just been delivered. My granddad, Harry Jackson, showed me the photo and the death notice on the front page of the paper.

He said, "Well, there goes another real old-timer. You remember when we talked with him at Ignacio two years ago?"

I remembered it well. We had gone to a picnic at Ute Memorial Park near the Ute Agency north of Ignacio. Harry Jackson had spotted the aged Buckskin Charley seated in a chair in the shade of a big cottonwood tree, and we had walked over to say hello. He greeted us with a wave and a handshake. He wore white-man's clothes—the Levis of the time—and a big brown cowboy hat. I thought he didn't look much like an Indian chief, but my grandfather assured me he was.

"That Indian is the last of the great Ute chiefs."

Through the years the two men, Harry Jackson and Buckskin

Charley, had had many business dealings. Charley had bought farm implements and wagons from Jackson Hardware.

Everyone in the San Juan Basin knew him from the photographs that Lisle Updike, a Durango photographer, had taken of him through the years. Even if they'd never seen him in person, they knew what he looked like. He personified the power of an old-time war chief with the wisdom of a statesman.

Official Ute records show that Buckskin Charley was born Charles Buck near Colorado Springs in 1840. However, some historians think he was probably born near Ignacio on the present-day Southern Ute Reservation, and others believe it more likely that he was born at the Ute Agency near Tierra Amarilla, New Mexico. Bob Delaney, former director of the Center for Southwest Studies at Fort Lewis College, and a friend who has helped me a great deal with this book, leans toward the Ignacio birthplace.

Charley became the leader of the Muache band of Utes who ranged over northern New Mexico away from their one-time agencies at Abiquiu and Tierra Amarilla. They raided and fought all over the eastern plains of New Mexico far beyond Cimmaron. It's possible, but not likely, that Charley participated in the Ute raids on the wagon trains traveling the Santa Fe Trail. The warlike Utes were a constant threat for a number of years to travelers on the Trail.

At the time of his birth, Ute bands roamed Colorado fighting Apaches, Comanches, Navajos, and Anglos for dominion. The United States government guaranteed in an 1868 treaty that most of western Colorado would be designated a Ute Reservation "for all time," which was before the discovery of silver and gold, of course. Utes, gold, prospectors, and miners didn't mix. The Utes had to go. Treaties were broken and new ones written, only to be broken or amended. Each time the Ute domain was a little smaller and the Utes were forced farther west. After the Meeker Massacre in September 1879, the Southern Utes were finally forced to resettle on two small reservations in the southwestern corner of Colorado and a small reservation, the Uintah–Ouray, in eastern Utah. They had been forced out of the New Mexico Territory a year before. Today the Southern Utes at Ignacio and the Ute Mountain Utes at Towaoc, south of Cortez, are Colorado's only Indian tribes.

Some scholars and historians say Buckskin Charley spoke only fair English, and others say he spoke no English. He seems to have been able to communicate in Spanish. Photographer Lisle Updike, not a Ute speaker, photographed him many times through the years from the early 1900s until 1936 and apparently had no trouble communicating with him.

People who knew Charley well say that his skin was a reddish bronze in color, that he'd lost the sight in one eye, and that he was married three times. He was said to have never forgotten a face and seldom a name.

He was a much admired man because he had taken the lead in teaching his people the "white man's way." At the same time he urged his people to preserve their language, their heritage, and their ceremonies. His religion was a mixture of Protestant, Catholic, and Ute. Without his leadership many of the old ceremonies might have been discarded and forgotten.

The *Durango News*, in an editorial shortly after his death, said of Buckskin Charley:

> The old-timers in this section were saddened to learn of the passing of Buckskin Charley, 99 (sic) year old chief of all the Utes. His death leaves the Ute Indians without a leader, and probably another will not be selected, at least not one to fill so preeminent a position as Buckskin did. With the coming of the White Man's way the chieftain idea is rapidly passing.
>
> Those who were acquainted with this old Indian are unanimous in their agreement that had Charley been a white man he would have been one of the nation's leaders, for he is generally considered one of the most intelligent red men in history.
>
> In such great esteem was he held as an Indian leader, that he was called to Washington by five different presidents to confer on matters pertaining to western Indians. He was present at the Inauguration of Theodore Roosevelt on March 4, 1905.

Chief Ouray was recognized by the U. S. as the principal Ute chief in the treaty of 1868. About 1870, Ouray designated Charlie as chief of the Muache band of Utes and as such made him a sub-chief of all the Utes. Charley accompanied Ouray and other chiefs to Washington in 1880.

Buckskin Charley, ca. 1880, member of the Indian Police at Ignacio.

Ouray died at Ignacio shortly after the Washington trip. On the third day of his illness Ouray summoned Charley to his bedside and named him successor. After Ouray's burial, in a secret place not far from Ignacio, Charley served as chief of the Muaches. Severo, a friend of Ouray's and Buckskin Charley, became chief of the Capote Utes. Ignacio, another trusted friend, became the chieftain for the Weeminuche band. All of this maneuvering was apparently necessary to prevent hostilities between the followers of the various strongmen.

In 1925 the Utes at Ignacio wanted to reinter the remains of Chief Ouray in the new Ute Memorial Park near Ignacio. Only Buckskin Charley had the authority to divulge the secret burial place and he led the official party to the spot where he had helped bury Ouray forty-five years earlier.

In his later years, Charley lived on his land near Ignacio. He tried to show the Southern Utes the advantage of farming and livestock breeding as opposed to gathering and hunting. He preached the futility of continued raids on Anglo settlements, and was generally credited for leading the warlike Utes on a path toward peace.

He is buried in the Ute Memorial Park with his old friends Ouray, Ignacio, and Severo. Charley's oldest son, Antonio Buck, succeeded him as chief. Antonio led the transition from the chieftain system to the present tribal council with elected officers. With the death of Buckskin Charley all vestiges of hereditary tribal leadership vanished.

My most vivid memory of Charley was in the summer of 1935. The Durango Chamber of Commerce and the Ute Tribe had organized a small barbecue at picnic grounds on Ute land near the old Fort Lewis campus about fifteen miles west of Durango. My parents were invited. As I recall, the county commissioners were included along with various state dignitaries. A delegation of Utes was expected to attend and everyone thought they would drive in from Ignacio or Towaoc.

It was late in the afternoon when we drove the 1933 Buick to the campground. A fire had been started and several people were busy preparing the meal. I spotted some kids my age and went over to join them in a game of catch. I have been unable to find a written account of this meeting. I know that it happened and that I was

Buckskin Charley, ca. 1920, with "peace medal." Photo by Lisle Updike.

there. I'm sure the year was 1935 as my father had had surgery in July and was resting at home. Mother drove the car, and after we got to the picnic area Dad took it easy in a folding camp chair. If he had been feeling well, he would have been down on the La Plata casting a fly rather than visiting with people around the campfire.

I must have played catch for an hour or more. The sun was down and the air had a fall nip. A number of cars had arrived, and I suppose there might have been fifty to sixty people gathered around in the shelter where the food was to be served.

I heard my mother calling me, "Jackson! Come quick!"

I ran toward the shelter and she pushed me along to the edge of the crowd that had gathered. "Look! That's Buckskin Charley riding into camp with his braves."

I could see a number of mounted Indians, six or more in single file, riding their horses bareback toward the campground. They were all decked out in feathered war bonnets, their faces painted an array of colors, each carrying a bow and arrow. Sure enough, leading the group on a big black horse was Buckskin Charley. His wrinkled face was emotionless, and his eyes were focused on the distance. He led the horsemen, who fifty years before would have been called warriors, in a circle around the campsite and then stopped and gave the command to dismount.

A man from the Chamber whispered to my Dad, "We thought they would be coming in in cars. We didn't expect this."

Two young Utes helped the aged chief dismount. I wormed my way to the front of the crowd to get a good look at the fabled leader. I was surprised how old he looked and how short he was. He was quite heavy and had great difficulty in walking.

By this time it was almost dark and the meal was ready to be served. Charley spoke with a white man, who might have been Hans Aspaas from Breen and a trusted advisor to the Utes.

The white man indicated that it was time for the "ceremony" and asked that a small fire be started away from the main shelter. It didn't take but a few minutes for the fire to blaze. The meal was postponed, but it didn't matter, all thoughts of food had evaporated. I watched Buckskin Charley and the Utes who had gathered around him. Few words were spoken and those only between the white man and a chamber of commerce representative and Buckskin Charley.

Finally the fire was ready. Buckskin Charley and the Utes sat crosslegged on the ground next to each other in a semicircle with Charley facing the river. The others were seated to his left, their faces illuminated only by the flames from the fire. Everyone was silent. The only sounds were the crackling fire and the river rush.

The white man motioned for the people from Durango, Denver, and other towns to sit in a semicircle on the other side of the fire facing west. He squatted next to Buckskin Charley, and in English said that we were gathered at the invitation of Buckskin Charley to commemorate many years of peace and friendship with his white neighbors. As a symbol of this friendship, everyone seated around the fire would smoke a peace pipe. He repeated this in the Ute language. Buckskin Charley nodded his head in agreement.

A pipe was lit and given to Charley who took a long drag. Smoke curled from the pipe as he passed it to a brave on his left and then to the white man on his right and around the circle to all who were seated there. The crowd remained silent. When everyone at the circle had smoked the pipe, it was passed to Buckskin Charley one last time. He passed it to the white man. Two braves helped Charley get on his feet and they walked beside him to the horses.

The meal still hadn't been served, but dinner was the last thing on anyone's mind. The old chief, Buckskin Charley, was leaving. The Utes led the horses close to the ceremonial fire and helped Charley mount. Then the chief and his followers rode away into the darkness. It was Buckskin Charley's last ride.

Harold Baxter Liebler, Priest to the Navajo

Harold Baxter Liebler, Episcopal priest, entered my life when he walked into Jackson Hardware on a bitter cold evening in February 1946. I learned later that he had come west in 1943 to bring Christ to the Navajos in the remote Utah Strip of the reservation. He and I were friends until his death in 1982.

Liebler came into the store just before closing time. He smiled and introduced himself. "I'm Father Liebler from St. Christopher's Mission in Bluff, Utah. I've come to pick up the order I called in."

Liebler, a tall, striking, middle-aged man, dressed in a long clerical cassock, a heavy, navy peacoat, and a black felt hat, was an imposing figure. His lined face, almost purple from the cold, showed the effects of sun and wind. I had not met Liebler. But my friends in Durango often described him as a "saint if there ever was one." I wanted to see what kind of man deserved that special praise.

We had Liebler's order all ready. He and I worked quickly in the biting winter weather loading pipe, rebars, nails, and roofing onto a topless, beat-up, bent-up, used-up surplus army carry-all. The cold pentrated my heavy coat, and it was well after dark when we finished. The street lights of Durango's Main Avenue, filtered through the driving snow, cast weird moving shadows on the nearly deserted street.

We returned, shivering, to the warm store where I took a good look at this man for the first time. He wore his graying hair tied Navajo style in a knot called *tsii'eel*, or "hair load," behind his head. I learned later the Navajos named him Ee'nishoodi bitsii' nez, "drag robe with long hair." He stood tall and straight as a poplar tree. I estimated him to be probably in his mid-fifties. I thought, "If he had a haircut and wasn't dressed in the black outfit he would really be a handsome man." I liked him immediately.

"Father," I said, "I've been going to Bluff since I was a youngster. I didn't know about an Episcopal mission there. I thought Bluff was a hundred percent Mormon. How long have you lived there?"

"Almost three years now. It's a long story, and we don't have time for it tonight. I have a long drive back to Bluff."

I walked him to the loading dock. He walked directly into the freezing wind, which was blowing harder and harder. Brushing the snow from the driver's seat in the unheated vehicle, he climbed in, and drove off into the storm. Alone in the open cab, he headed for Bluff, two hundred miles away.

The snow fell in waves; visibility approached zero; bone-chilling cold pierced my parka like a knife. The storm reminded me of the previous winter, 1945, when I fought in the Battle of the Bulge and had frozen my feet. I hated cold weather.

I thought, "He has to be some kind of a crazy old guy," and dismissed him from my mind. But I wondered what motivated him. After that evening, I saw him occasionally when he came to Durango. Sometimes he shopped at our store; sometimes I would see him having coffee with the local Episcopal priest.

In 1949 or 1950 I went to Bluff on business. I stopped at Cow Canyon Trading Company and met Brother Juniper, who worked with Liebler at St. Christopher's. He was a pleasant, gregarious fellow garbed in a tattered cassock but not as tall as Liebler. I judged him to be in his mid-forties. His name was Hillyer Ford, but most folks knew him as Brother Juniper, an Episcopal Franciscan monk, who had joined Father Liebler to work with the Navajo.

I drove to the mission, located two miles east of Bluff. St. Christopher's is a lovely place, nestled against the towering sandstone cliffs that form a plateau above the San Juan River. Aged cottonwoods grew on the riverbank and within the mission compound.

There I saw Liebler, attired in his customary black cassock, walking toward a building that I later learned was the chapel. He stopped to greet me.

"Welcome to St. Christopher's. I'm Father Liebler. I see you have Colorado plates, Durango, isn't it?"

"I see you in Durango once in a while. I'm Jackson Clark from Jackson Hardware. We've met several times before. I want to learn more about St. Christopher's."

We chatted as we strolled toward the log chapel building, constructed in the shape of a cross in a grove of trees. Liebler stopped outside the chapel and suggested we rest on a bench shaded by a large cottonwood tree. The shade was a welcome refuge from the ovenlike desert sun. A light breeze blew up the river, and the leaves shimmered in a rhythymless dance. When Liebler began to speak I relaxed and listened. Suddenly time didn't matter, getting home in time for dinner didn't matter. Only this man and his lonely mission mattered.

He began, "The Utah Strip is a piece of Utah, mostly on the Navajo Reservation. It's been neglected and forgotten for many years by the U. S. Government, the State of Utah, and even the Navajo Tribe. The Utah Strip is all the land north of the Arizona line and south of the San Juan River. Bluff and the mission are just north of the river, just off the reservation. There are many Navajo families living there. I don't think anyone knows how many, but we serve several hundred and there must be a thousand or more."

Born in Brooklyn in 1889, Liebler had lived mostly in New York and New England. He had been the rector in a peaceful parish in Old Greenwich, Connecticut, before moving to Utah.

He said, "I have always been fascinated with the American Indian. I even learned a bit of the Navajo lauguage many years ago. For one reason or another I began studying them, their culture, and their language. As you probably know, the Navajo language is quite difficult. It's an Asian language, and our rules of grammar, pronunciation, and sentence structure don't apply. It is a tongue of subtle sounds. Words seem to come from the throat and the nose all at the same time. It is also an expressive language rich in vocabulary and ideas. I learned it first from a book."

He visited Utah on a trip in 1942, riding a borrowed Navajo

pony, and witnessed the poor living conditions of the Navajo people.

"I found there were no churches, no schools, and no medical care. I wrote home and told my parish that I must move here. There was a need for me. It was unbelievable that human beings were living such pitiful lives in our great country."

Liebler sincerely felt the need to do something for the Navajo. His reaction stands out in sharp contrast to that of many non-Indians, most of whom are put off by Indian customs and living conditions and wish to do nothing more than to forget them. Liebler asked the Episcopal Bishop of Utah for permission to establish a mission near Bluff. He said that the Bishop did not know part of the Navajo Tribe was in Utah and thus under his jurisdiction. Once convinced, he gave Liebler permission to found St. Christopher's. Liebler understood from the start that money was tight and that he was mostly on his own.

As we sat there I heard the roar of the San Juan River, near flood stage from melting snows in the Colorado mountains. It plunged westward past Bluff toward its rendezvous with the Colorado River a hundred miles beyond in the Utah desert canyons. Sandstone cliffs towered over the tiny stone mission buildings. Billowing, ever-changing clouds dotted the turquoise blue sky. The leaves whispered. The river, the setting, the trees, and Father Liebler's faith emphasized that we are God's creatures and dwarfed by His creation.

Liebler continued, "I knew that a mission was needed but would be difficult to establish because Bluff is so isolated. The roads are bad when it rains, and not much better when it doesn't. But I felt compelled to build the mission to serve the Navajo, body and spirit. I didn't think that I could preach the gospel to the hungry and poorly clothed without trying to improve their lot in life. I wanted to give them hope for the present and future. It's my life's work: sometimes tiring, disappointing, and discouraging, but we're making progress."

"Father," I asked, "How were you received by the People, the Navajo?"

"Well, it was slow going for a long time. I suppose that they came to services more out of curiosity than anything else. The first Sunday we were here, in the summer of 1943, Brother Michael, Helen

Father Liebler, ca. 1955.

Sturges, and the others who came with me gathered for Mass. Two Navajo children sat on their horse watching from the hillside. The next Sunday a Navajo family hid behind the sagebrush and took in the entire service. From that date on we never celebrated Mass without Navajos, even if only watched from a distance.

"Preaching the gospel and trying to establish a school and a clinic and to gain trust and understanding is one thing. Having the Navajo accept the word of God and a belief in Christ is quite another. Imagine, if you can, telling people of Christ and the Resurrection—His rising from the dead—when their greatest fear is the dead, including objects and places associated with death. I had to do a real selling job to convince any Navajo that Jesus was his savior too. Navajos have no fear of dying, but they fear dead people and the objects which belonged to the deceased. Most Navajos will not even look upon the dead."

I listened intently as he went on, "Navajos will not even eat rabbit. Why? Because rabbits live in the rocks under the cliffs and this is where many Navajos are buried. To eat a rabbit is like eating a creature that might be inhabited by the ghost of a relative or friend. The Navajo people have strong beliefs in the supernatural.

"Finally on an Easter Sunday, several years after we arrived here, a Navajo family came to decorate a child's grave. It was the first time that any family from here had ever visited a grave."

Liebler smiled as he continued, "The youngster died in a hogan fire and had been buried in our little cemetery near the mission. The family had not been present at the funeral. Only our little group here at St. Christopher's had been there. But now the family came to visit the grave. From then on I knew that in addition to the physical things we did for them, like providing food, clothing, and health care, they wanted to know Christ. We had always prayed that this would happen, and this instance gave us a sign that we were making progress. It was a joyful day."

Liebler and I left the cottonwood's shade and walked to the chapel. The altar, which he had built with his own hands, was of native stone; rough wooden benches provided seats for about twenty persons. Navajo rugs woven with crosses and "Jesus" hung from the walls and lay on the floor in front of the altar.

"Navajos are slow to change, but we have plenty of time, so this

High altar at St. Christopher's.

is all right with us. I conduct the services and give the sermons in Navajo. We use Navajo rugs, as you can see, to decorate the building. The altar is freestanding, so I never turn my back on the congregation as I prepare the sacraments. To turn one's back on a Navajo is a sign of great disrespect."

I discovered later that he had not requested financial aid from the Executive Council of the Episcopal Church because he respected the Navajos' rights to engage in their traditional tribal ceremonies. The Council had an official policy to discourage or actually forbid participation by baptized Navajos. Indeed, the official policy of the Church mandated that Navajos cut and trim their long hair. Liebler grew his hair long.

St. Christopher's had the only clinic within a hundred miles and also a small school. Liebler explained, "We do more than just bring Christ into their lives. We try to heal their bodies too. Doctors and nurses come frequently, on a *pro bono* basis, for well-baby clinics, physical exams, and the like. I don't know what we would do without them."

Reluctantly, I returned to Durango. My first visit to St. Christopher's had been an eye-opener. On subsequent visits to Bluff I learned about Liebler's missions at Navajo Mountain and Oljeto, near Monument Valley. Liebler and his crew saw the need for a mission in the Monument Valley area and established Our Lady of the Moonlight near the Oljeto trading post, not far from John Wetherill's original store. The first chapel was a hogan. I have always thought the mission brought sunlight into the drab lives of the poverty-stricken Indians. Several years later the Mission was renamed Hat Rock, after a distinctive rock formation that towered over the area. Liebler visited Navajo Mountain on a monthly basis for many years. Other denominations had churches in that remote mountain area, but Liebler felt there was a need for an Episcopal mission.

On one of my first trips to St. Christopher's I met Helen Sturges, a soft-spoken, pretty woman, who had come to Utah with Liebler. Later on I met Joan Eskell, a tall, strikingly handsome British woman, who became Liebler's wife in later years.

There seemed to be a certain competition between the two women. In subtle, indefinable ways there was an ongoing struggle for Father Liebler's attention and praise. This had no visible effect on St. Christopher's work, however. Whatever competition existed between Joan and Helen, the entire crew, including volunteers from all over the country, worked in unison.

Brother Juniper, always at hand, ever ready with a kind word and some obscure piece of historical knowledge, became one of my close friends. Helen and Joan were lay people. Brother Juniper and Brother Michael, who had arrived earlier in the year, were from the American Order of St. Francis, and had volunteered to work with Liebler in the Utah Strip. (After retirement Brother Juniper returned to Wisconsin and married his childhood sweetheart. He died in 1991.)

I always stopped at St. Christopher's on my frequent trips to the reservation. The most enjoyable visit I made each year came shortly before Christmas. I drove a van to St. Christopher's loaded with soft drinks, frozen turkeys, cakes, clothing and toys, and other holiday goodies. In later years, after Liebler, Juniper, Joan and Helen had "retired" and moved to Oljeto, I drove my Christmas load to Hat Rock.

The congregation of St. Mark's in Durango collected canned goods, warm clothing, toys, and games for me to take. The Bonan brothers, who owned Vita Kist Bakery in Cortez, donated a dozen or more freshly baked sheet cakes for this annual event. (Years later they baked the wedding cake I took to Liebler and Joan shortly after their marriage.) I felt like a true Santa as I sped across the desert on my journey to the mission.

I will never receive a warmer, more appreciative welcome anytime, anywhere. Liebler told me that I was an answer to their prayers. I would look around the meager quarters the little band called home and be thankful that I could help. I felt so inadequate, so humble on many of these visits. But the satisfaction of having helped in some small way lasted beyond Christmas Day.

One time I was just north of Kayenta when I had a feeling that I should slow down and approach a small rise in the road with caution. Everything seemed okay, but I sensed danger. On the far side of the hill an eighteen-wheeler cattle truck had jackknifed across the road, and I would have plowed into it. I mentioned this to Liebler on my next visit. He smiled and said, "Our Lord works many miracles, if we will let Him be with us."

St. Christopher's has grown much since 1943. Next to the chapel and the Mission House, a vicarage, an eight-bed clinic, a schoolhouse, and several work buildings and dormitories have been built. Tragically, the original log chapel was destroyed in a fire intentionally set by a deranged individual who thought Liebler pandered to the Navajo by preaching in Navajo and not forbidding native ceremonies. However, the silver chalice and paten, brought from Connecticut years before, survived the heat of the fire. They were the only items recovered from the ruins of the lovely little chapel. Liebler said that this sign confirmed he was indeed on the right course.

In 1966 Father Liebler, Brother Juniper, Helen Sturges, and Joan moved to the Hat Rock Mission and Retreat Center, near the original Hogan mission of St. Mary of the Moonlight. I learned later

Joan Liebler and Father Liebler (l.) shortly after their marriage. Brother Juniper and Helen Sturges on right.

that Father Liebler had purchased the small tract of land many years before from the Utah School Land Board. They lived in a rickety old two-story building that leaned precariously to the north, as if to protect itself from the bitter wind that whipped the canyon in winter. The living quarters, located on the second floor, were cramped and uncomfortable. The ground floor was used for storage of food and clothing to be given to the Navajos. Directly behind the building was a small laundry room with two wringer-type washers, for Navajo use.

Liebler worked in a small office at the front of the building, his desk piled high with papers. He laughingly told me he was "getting my desk organized. It looks a mess, but everything is here, right at my fingertips." Soon after Liebler, Helen, Joan, and Juniper moved to Hat Rock, they built a small chapel a short distance from the house. A Navajo stonemason constructed it of native red rock. The walls are twenty-four inches thick.

Joan Liebler overseeing the laundry room.

Liebler, Juniper, Helen, and Joan had all reached retirement age when they moved to Hat Rock. Brother Juniper told me, "We're all on Social Security, and here we're starting a new life." And a new life it was, complex and tiring, the work most demanding, the Navajos no better off than those who lived near Bluff. To make matters worse, most charitable contributions still went to St. Christopher's. Hat Rock had to stand alone, and it took years to construct a new financial base. I marveled at Helen's tenacity in scrounging up used car parts to repair their aging vehicles. Everything was patchwork except the church building.

I visited Hat Rock frequently, more than four hundred fifty miles round trip from Durango. The spiritual lift I gained on each visit easily made up for the trip. Nevertheless, it was a sorely deprived group that held the mission together. On several occasions I brought new wringer-type washing machines for use in the laundry room. Though the water quality was excellent, the supply was limited. Automatic washers would use too much water. Joan took charge of the laundry and kept the machines running long after most people would have given up, and the machines seemed to run constantly. Joan explained, "The Navajo children have to have clean clothes. They ride the bus to Monticello to school every day, and they are in classes with Mormon kids who tend to look down on them anyway. Washing clothes in a muddy arroyo just won't do."

One Christmas Father Liebler asked me about Durango and his friends there. "I miss seeing some of the people I have known for years," he said. "But I guess that they have mostly forgotten me anyway."

Certainly many of the friends from the early days at Bluff were dead and gone, but others in Durango and Cortez always remembered him. By the late 1970s Liebler had become a legend. He was being "discovered" and received many more visitors than in the early years. But the financial resources were still sorely taxed. Joan worked diligently on a newsletter drumming up moral and financial support. Helen transported sick and dying Navajos to the hospital. Juniper kept things running while representing San Juan County on the State Tourism Board. The older they got, the more active they became.

Each visit to Hat Rock turned into an adventure. One morning I arrived to find Father and Helen deep in a conversation regarding an aged Navajo woman who had died the night before. She had died of a lingering illness in the family hogan. Helen had spent the night with the family taking care of the body and getting help from neighbors. I asked her, "Helen, when a person dies like that isn't the hogan deserted or burned?"

"Yes, that's true if the death is sudden, or if it's a younger person. Mrs. Begay was over ninety years old. The Navajos say, 'Oh, she didn't die. Her life is just over.' That is the way they look at it, and that is what I believe too."

I asked Liebler how he dealt with Navajos who believed in witchcraft. It took him a long time to answer. "I teach that there is only one God and that Jesus Christ is our savior. Much of this is not compatible with Navajo religion. What is called Navajo religion is actually a group of myths and beliefs that are very beautiful and inspiring, but which, in the long run, give no hope for what lies ahead of a person after this life. There is no hope of anything better. But from the very beginning at St. Christopher's I never discouraged Navajo beliefs, I never told them to stop the ceremonies or so-called sings. I respect them and their beliefs and want to make them aware of Jesus without being evangelistic and dogmatic.

"When we first went to Bluff the local Mormons would have almost nothing to do with a Navajo. This has changed now, and there are many active Mormon missionaries on the reservation. But in the beginning, back in 1943, what we saw was scorn for the Navajo because of skin color. The Mormons took their money but considered the Navajo inferior. We gave dignity to each person as an individual."

"I know that, Father, but have you ever had a person come to you who had been, or thought they had been, witched?"

"People used to say that they saw skinwalkers around. I never saw one, but I know that they are here. I don't believe that they are supernatural creatures or even superhuman beings. I think they are just malevolent people who have a grudge or resentment against a Navajo or his family, and get dressed in an animal skin in order to scare the daylights out of the poor souls. Mostly it is brought on by jealousy and envy.

"One time, several years ago, a lady came to the mission, right here at Hat Rock, and said that skinwalkers came to her hogan almost every night. They climbed on the roof and dropped unmentionable articles down the smoke hole. They terrified her. I talked to her and told her that I would pray with her and give her something to frighten the creatures away. We prayed together and when we had finished I gave her a small jar of holy water. I told her to wait until the skinwalker looked down the smoke hole of the hogan's roof, then pray silently for him to go away. At the same time she should throw the water in his face and say, 'Go! Go! In the name of Jesus Christ, go, and never return!' She followed my instructions, and she saw no more trouble.

"We all have to believe in something, and the power of Christ is bigger and more powerful than that of a skinwalker or witch. I believe in Jesus Christ, and He is the supreme power. I have believed since I was a teenager doing chores in a church. As I remember, I wasn't too happy about working when my friends were out playing ball. I looked up at the altar one day and saw a light and felt a presence in that building. I fell to my knees, full of joy and happiness. I said to myself, 'It's real! I know He is real.' From that day on I have dedicated myself to Him. You see, there is no reason for me to believe in the power of skinwalkers." As he spoke, tears ran down his face and he took my hand in both of his. It was a powerful moment.

Another Christmas in the late 1970s, I took my usual load of goods to Hat Rock. Father asked, "Is it awfully dry up there, too, Jackson? We need snow badly here in the desert."

I told him that it was grim in Colorado too. The ski areas had not opened because of little or no snowfall in the mountains. "I heard the Vail ski resort hired a band of Southern Utes to do a snow dance. Fat lot of good that will do, don't you think, Father?"

He studied his cluttered desk for a moment and then looked at me with his penetrating eyes and said, "Oh, I don't know. Our Lord listens to many drums. Perhaps he will hear this one."

That night it snowed in Vail. I called him the next day and told him about the storm. Southern Utah and the Durango area were still dry. I could hear him chuckle as he said, "Maybe the Utes have a special power in their drums."

I think of the thousands of tourists who visited Goulding's

Lodge, just a few miles away in Monument Valley. Only a few of them ever visited Hat Rock to meet Father Liebler. Few of the tour guides at Goulding's stopped by to see what was happening. I was the fortunate one. The whole experience changed my life and gave me a faith that I had never had.

Several things stand out in my memory about the Mission at Hat Rock. The most memorable was the baptism of my grandson, Edward, in May of 1981, when he was five months old. I telephoned Father Liebler to tell him we wanted to bring Edward over. He was delighted. "Of course, Jackson, bring everyone on Saturday, and we'll get the young man off to a good start in life. Helen and Joan are both away so you will have to put up with Brother Juniper and me."

We left Durango bright and early on a sunny June day. We first stopped in Farmington to load a new washing machine for Hat Rock. Finally we were off for Oljeto. I have never seen the desert as lovely as on that day. The early summer flowers bloomed, the grass grew tall and waved in the wind. Clouds dotted the sky, and there was no hint of rain.

We arrived at Oljeto before eleven in the morning and unloaded the washing machine while we did the paper work. Father Liebler was terribly lame. Brother Juniper was not much better. Our little band, eager to get Edward off to a good start, filed into the Hat Rock church. It was high noon but cool and dark in the chapel.

Father Liebler took Edward in his arms, blessed him with holy water, and handed him to Brother Juniper. At that moment all hell broke loose. Edward, having been rudely awakened from a sound sleep by the splash of water, set up a terrible howl. Father Liebler and Brother Juniper went on as if they didn't hear a thing. The words of the baptismal liturgy were obliterated by the merciless screeching of Edward Jackson Clark. At one point he settled down, looked all around, and just whimpered a bit. About that time there was another splash of water, and he was off again. Father Liebler and Brother Juniper, two old men of the cloth, both wearing magnifying glasses in order to read the scripture, cradled Edward as he continued to scream, his eyes wide with fear.

After the baptism, Father Liebler said, "That's all right. It got the Devil out of him for all time. I must say he has a healthy set of lungs."

During lunch, Father Liebler and Brother Juniper were at their best, telling stories of the early days in Bluff, the difficulties they encountered building the mission and imparting the word of Christ to the Navajo. It was one of the last days we spent with them.

Father Liebler died in November 1982. He was ninety-seven. He had not been well for some time but remained active to the end. Finally his gallant spirit just gave up.

The funeral was to be held at Hat Rock with burial at St. Christopher's. We made plans to go. It was a bright, cold, windy day at Oljeto. The stone chapel was packed to overflowing with Navajos and others from far and near. Brother Juniper described the mood when I asked him how he was doing. "Oh, we're doing okay, but we're leaking around the seams. There are lots of tears and sadness here, Jackson, but lots of joy too, because we had so many years together."

Catholic and Episcopal priests, several Methodist ministers, and preachers from other denominations came to pay a last tribute to a man who had given most of his life for the Navajo people. Most spoke in Navajo, the language of the mission. Father Liebler would have been proud to see Father Plummer, a Navajo he had trained, participating in the service. Father Plummer became the rector of St. Christopher's a few years later, and now is the Bishop for the Episcopal church in Navajoland.

Fifty or more cars headed for the burial site at St. Christopher's after the service. I paid particular attention to how the reservation looked that day. Navajo Mountain rose far to the west, shrouded in the blue-gray haze of autumn. The desert looked deceptively warm and welcoming, but the air seemed cold and the wind blew steadily from the north. The chamisa plants beside the highway, only now beginning to lose the yellow blossoms of fall, bobbed and waved as the cars rolled by. I remember thinking that even the plants were saying farewell.

We crossed the San Juan River at Mexican Hat and proceeded on over Comb Ridge into Bluff. My mind was full of memories of Liebler, and I wondered how many times he had made this same trip on a mission to serve his beloved Navajo.

The original church site of St. Christopher's was empty, still marked by foundation stones arranged in the form of the cross.

The grave was within the foundation in the right-hand wing of the cross. Everyone gathered around the open grave. It was November 27, and all the leaves had fallen from the cottonwoods except one old tree, its leaves still bright green. It stood over Liebler's grave like a sentry, watching and waiting for his return. A light breeze blew as the Navajo pallbearers bore the coffin to the site and prepared to lower it into the grave.

Father Plummer chanted in Navajo, tears streaking his brown face. The casket disappeared into the grave. I watched the faces of the Navajos. Young and old alike wept. All those present knew they had lost a true friend, but there was a feeling of peace in the place. An era had come to an end. Father Liebler was gone.

A Navajo man shoveled the first bit of dirt onto the casket. At that moment the wind began to blow. The temperature dropped fifteen degrees in a few minutes. I wrapped my jacket tightly around my shoulders and looked up at the tall cottonwood. One by one, then five by five, ten by ten, and hundreds by hundreds the leaves began to fall. A dust devil rolled across the parking lot. I felt a powerful presence. I looked at the tree, now stripped bare of leaves, but green only moments before. The feeling of God's love was almost overpowering. The wind died down in a matter of minutes and all was calm. Father Liebler was at peace with his Maker.

Trading Pepsi for Navajo Rugs, 1957

I grew up with Navajo rugs. We had them at home and at the cabin. We used them but never considered them to be works of art. They were rugs to be walked on or used to hide the tattered fabric on a couch or sofa. When the rugs became worn and threadbare we used them as door mats. They were cheap, plentiful, and only moderately interesting. When I went to New Mexico Military Institute I took several Navajo rugs along for my room.

My parents were interested in the Navajo as individuals and artists but never collected Navajo crafts as an art form. On our frequent reservation trips we'd stop to visit a weaver and sometimes Dad would trade hardware items for a rug. The rugs we bought and didn't use we gave away or sold.

After I came home from the army I began to learn about rugs and how to determine value. My father-in-law, Ed Black of Blanco, New Mexico, a respected trader, taught me a few things starting in 1947. I learned to watch for straight lines, pleasing designs, and quality work.

When my family sold Jackson Hardware Company in 1957, I went to work as sales manager for the Pepsi-Cola Bottling Company in Durango. Because I knew many of the traders, Dave McGraw, the owner, wanted me to spend much of my time on the Navajo Reservation. Pepsi lagged far behind Coca-Cola in reservation sales.

My third day on the job, May 3, 1957, Dave asked me to go to a trading post south of Shiprock to collect an overdue account. Dave said, "I think you might know the trader. We just can't get any money from him. Right now he owes us twenty-five hundred dollars. Go down and see what you can do. He won't answer my letters and refuses to take a phone call. You can collect that bill, I know you can."

I welcomed the opportunity and took off early the following morning, full of confidence, maybe a little cocky. I did indeed know the trader. I had purchased a fine Two Grey Hills rug from him several years before, but I hadn't seen him since.

"You can count on me."

Dave smiled and said, "Good! I knew you could do it."

I thought to myself that I must have landed the best of all possible jobs. Here I was working and doing what I liked best—going to the reservation.

My optimism vanished when I drove up to the store. The screen door, hanging by one hinge, twisted in the wind. The store was filthy. The cash register drawer was open as if to say, "There's no money here." A dozen or more Navajo men sat in the sun outside the door waiting for the railroad retirement man to come by and sign them up. They had all worked on railroad construction during the previous year. A few dusty cans of Spam, beans, and coffee sat on the otherwise bare shelves. To top it off, my old friend was drunk.

"Hi there," I said, "Do you remember me? I am with Pepsi now and came down to collect twenty-five hundred dollars you owe Mr. McGraw."

He scowled and then growled out his answer. "Yeah, I remember you. You're that Clark kid, aren't you? Well, you are barking up the wrong tree if you want money. This place is broke. Look at it." He gave a sweeping wave of his hand for emphasis.

"Come on back in my living quarters and have a drink."

"Wow! It's only ten o'clock in the morning. I don't want a drink, but I'd take a Pepsi or something."

"We don't have any Coke or Pepsi. The place is broke, I tell you it's broke. How would I buy Pepsi?"

Completely discouraged, I followed him into his living quarters behind the store. As I passed through the storage room I saw a neat stack of Navajo rugs.

"I've got an idea. Let me take some of those rugs and give you credit—if you give me a good deal—and we'll settle the bill. What do you say?"

He poured himself a shot of bourbon and stroked his chin. "Would you really do that?"

"Sure, I know a good one from a bad one, and these look like they are all fine weavings."

"Okay, we got a deal. I'll make you a good price. Just get them together and let me know. I'm going to take a nap." He looked like hell.

I had all the rugs spread out when Sam, the Navajo clerk, came over to give me some advice.

"I don't think you ought to take that one. See how crooked it is? Let me help you."

Within an hour we had the stack of rugs I wanted, but they added up to thirty-five hundred dollars. About that time my friend got up from his nap. I explained the situation.

"Now what?" he asked.

I thought quickly. "Let me take the whole bunch. I'll credit the account for twenty-five hundred and give you credit for a thousand in Pepsi. We can send a truckload down tomorrow." We both thought we had made a fine bargain.

"Sounds good to me. Maybe I can get this place back on its feet again. What's McGraw going to say?"

"Don't worry about Dave. I'll handle him." Famous last words.

The drive back to Durango was wonderful. I had made a good deal and I knew it. I had no idea what we'd do with the rugs, but at least I'd settled the bill.

Dave McGraw didn't see it that way. He hit the ceiling.

"You took *rugs* instead of getting cash? I can't believe that! He does that with everyone. You get up early tomorrow and take them back and get the money."

I was shocked. "Dave, there isn't any money. The place is broke. It's a mess."

"He has money. Just go down and get it. I'm really disappointed

Jackson Clark at Mexican Water Trading Post. Don Reeves, manager, poses with two weavers, 1968.

with you." He shot me a glance that chilled me to the soles of my feet and then walked out the door.

Dave and his wife, Hazel McGraw, were wonderful people. They had built their business from scratch and wanted it to continue to grow. Ilene (Sammy) McGraw, Dave's sister, did the books and bossed the help. The three of them made up a fine crew. They liked me and I liked them, but on that afternoon I thought that I was soon out of a job.

That evening my wife, Mary Jane, and I had a dinner party. I worried all during cocktails and dinner about the rugs. Dave just didn't understand the situation. I toyed briefly with the idea of calling him and suggesting that *he* take the rugs back but decided that would be a sure ticket out.

Gradually a plan came to mind. I looked around the table. The guests included two doctors, a prominent lawyer, and a banker. I began by offering coffee, then Irish coffee, then brandy, and a dessert wine.

Selecting Navajo rugs at Mexican Water.

"By the way, today I went to 'such-and-such' trading post and got a bunch of nice Navajo rugs. Would you all like to see them? I can bring them in from the car."

My timing was perfect. Our guests, relaxed by the meal and drinks, raved about the rugs, poring over them like bargain shoppers at Macy's. Before midnight I had sold all the rugs for a total of thirty-six hundred dollars, give or take a few. I'd made a good deal and so had my buyers. I had one condition: "You have to pay me tonight, right now." Then I told them the story.

"I can't charge them. I have to have cash or checks by 9:00 A.M. so I can settle up with Dave."

Money was no problem. Everyone came up with the cash. I got my thirty-six hundred dollars and changed it all into hundred-dollar bills as soon as the bank opened. I waited for McGraw in his office.

A few minutes after 9:00 Dave strolled in, looking a little the worse for wear. He didn't smile. "Why didn't you go back to the reservation? Why are you here?"

"Sit down for a minute, Dave. I have something for you."

He sat at his desk with his eyes fixed on me as I counted out twenty-five hundred-dollar bills and placed them in front of him. "That settles the bill the trader owed us."

Dave squinted at me, counted the money, then asked, "How'd you do that so soon?"

"I'll explain in a minute. Now, here's another thousand dollars. That's for Pepsi we are starting to deliver today." In 1957 a thousand dollars bought a lot of soft drinks.

"And Dave, here's a hundred for you."

Dave fingered the bill and smiled for the first time that day. He looked me straight in the eye and asked, "Can you do that again?"

I continued trading Navajo rugs for Pepsi until the 1970s, when we began to buy almost everything directly from the weavers. In the meantime Pepsi became the leading soft drink on the northern Navajo reservation.

I bought and sold several thousand rugs during those years, yet outside of the Durango Collection, I kept very few. Indeed, too few. But during this time I found my first love in weaving, Navajo pictorials.

Navajo Pictorial Rugs

There is magic in a Navajo pictorial rug. I discovered this magic many years ago when a trader sold me a small pictorial woven in bright commercial-dye colors. I was enchanted by the sense of tranquility woven into the rug. Unfortunately, I never even learned the weaver's name. At that time it didn't seem to matter; now it's important.

The scene depicted a Navajo hogan, sheep, cattle, birds, and a bright blue sky with billowing white clouds. This insignificant little pictorial held me. I was hooked, good and proper.

Frankly, before this I had always ignored Navajo contemporary pictorial weaving as being too modern, untraditional, and somewhat funky. But when I had hung my new pictorial on my office wall the details began to assert themselves. I saw a coffee pot on a cook fire, the skin of freshly butchered sheep hanging on a hitching post, and a woman spinning wool. Many times through the years I have looked at the rug, and a sense of peace and tranquility has come over me. It was an elixir for the care and stress of a busy day. Navajo weaving is a true American folk art, and pictorial weaving is its finest form.

My utterly captivating Navajo weaving got me started collecting pictorials. I learned to begin each visit to a trading post by looking at the pictorial rugs. The word soon got around among my trader friends that I was a sucker for a good pictorial, and I got the first chance to buy new items. I admire all Navajo weavers, but a good pictorial weaver absolutely gets me in the pocketbook.

I have been fascinated watching Navajo weavers at their looms creating rugs of exquisite quality from visions alone. Almost never are there drawings, sketches, or plans to follow. One weaver told me that she has only the roughest idea when she begins to weave. Another weaver said the process of formulating the design comes gradually as she washes, cards, and spins the wool in preparation for weaving. As an artist chooses colors from a palette, the Navajo weaver will choose from the wool colors available at the trading post, or, in the case of some weavers, dyestuff from plants, roots, and natural materials. Frequently the subject is chosen after the warp is strung on the loom and the weaving started.

One weaver told me, "I'm just going to do that plain bottom border today and then go home to sleep on it, and talk to my grandmother." I was a little surprised. We were at a museum in a large city, and I didn't think her grandmother had made the trip. In fact, I realized her grandmother was dead. I waited until the next morning to see what would happen. The weaver came in smiling and in good spirits and began to weave. After an hour or so I asked, "What did your grandmother say?"

"Oh, Grandmother told me to do a Squaw Dance scene with lots of people in it."

I mentioned to her that I thought that her grandmother was dead.

"Yes, that's right, she's been dead a long time. I talk to her in my dreams."

I'm not sure that all Navajo weavers talk to their dead grandmothers, but they receive inspiration from mysterious sources.

When I buy pictorials I buy what appeals to me and pay little attention to the criteria for quality that guide most buyers. I have bought crooked rugs and some rather ugly rugs because they jump from a rug pile and speak to me. Maybe the weaver's grandmother is talking to me. I know that something or someone is talking to me. When I fail to pay attention, I regret it for days.

Once in a while a pictorial weaver will bring a rug that is so unusual it can't be resisted. For example, I bought a rough little pictorial from a lady who took the few dollars I paid her and left in a

Isabel John at her loom.

hurry. I suspect she was glad to unload it on me. Many months later she returned, and I asked her about the scenes in the little rug.

"Alice, I can see that there is a horse or two tied to a tree, a hogan, and apparently a ceremony going on in the hogan. There are lots of pickup trucks and people, but what are those two black things and the black glob in the top panel?"

"Oh, that's easy. That's the Four Corners Power plant, and the black thing is a pile of coal. All the people are going to a Firedance ceremony in that hogan." It was as easy as that! The mystery ended, but the charm increased.

Customers ask about special ordering pictorials. This can be very tricky. If money is paid in advance, the quality may suffer, and there is the matter of dealing with cultural differences. Navajos don't necessarily see things the way we may assume they do. Sometimes voice and vision rather speak louder. Perfectly clear instructions to a fluent, English-speaking weaver may be totally misunderstood. This is true even when instructions are typed in large block letters. Many weavers speak no English and must rely on a friend or relative to translate and conduct business. In translation some things are lost. This is more understandable in light of reservation life. During the last forty years I have driven over almost every road and trail in Navajoland. I am always impressed at the isolation of some families, many of whom live without running water, modern plumbing, or electricity. The kids go to school, adults work, but the weavers stay home and weave. For many Navajo people, especially the oldsters, a trip to town is a real event, an occasion to dress up in the finest clothes and wear their best jewelry.

Gilbert Maxwell, in his book on Navajo weaving, tells of ordering a rug to advertise his business: "Gilbert Maxwell and Son, Farmington, New Mexico." When the rug was completed Farmington had become Framington.

"What's the difference?" asked the weaver. "Farmington, Framington, it's all the same." In Navajo, Farmington is Totah, where the three waters meet, and that is what counts. Farmington is just another white man's word.

I have fallen into this special-order trap many times. Most of the time everything works out okay, but sometimes it doesn't. Each time I give special instructions to a pictorial weaver, even one I have known for ages, I wonder to myself, "Is this really wise? How will it turn out?" Once, I ordered a small wall hanging as a gift for a friend. It was supposed to read, "Gilbert Balkin, Collector of Things." When the weaver brought it to my office Balkin had become Baiken and Collector had only one "l."

Recently I ordered a pictorial for a fiftieth wedding anniversary: "Jennings and Harriette, March 28, 1938." The weaver changed Harriette to Harrietts because "Harriette is such a funny way to spell a name." I think this happened because Navajos frequently misuse the generic plural by adding an 's.' Sheep become sheeps, cattle are cattles. Jennings and Harriettes liked the rug anyway.

I remember asking a weaver if she would weave an American flag. "Sure thing, no problem." And there was no problem. It was a superior work. Then I ordered a Colorado flag; again, no problem. Then she did a New Mexico flag. It was perfect.

"How about a Texas flag rug?" I asked.

"Balkin had become Baikin and collector had one L."

She said that it would be easy to do.

I furnished an actual flag for the rugs. How could I go wrong with a Texas flag, if I got a flag the same size as the rug I wanted to have woven? A few months passed, and I began to be concerned about my order. I wanted to take it to Midland for a show. I called the weaver's daughter who worked in an office with a phone. I asked when the Texas rug would be ready. She said that her mother was having "trouble with that star" but that it would be ready on Monday.

The moment the weaver and her extended family arrived in the showroom I knew something had gone wrong. The usually rowdy kids remained quiet and hid behind grandmother's skirts. Her daughter, the mother of the four kids, waited in the hall. The menfolk stayed in the pickup. Every time they had been up before, the entire family had come into the gallery. We always had a marvelous time,

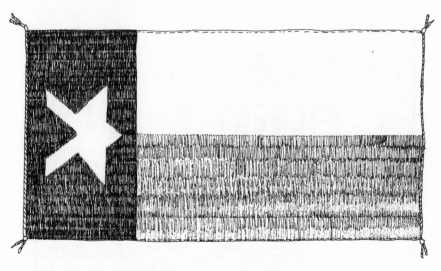

Texas flag rug. "She's been havin' trouble with that star."

telling jokes, sipping soft drinks, and bargaining over the price. Now something bothered her.

Esther, the weaver, was sad. She was frightened and apprehensive, too. Everyone sensed it. A tear ran down her cheek as she clutched the still unseen rug, wrapped in a Cortez Milling Company flour sack, tucked tightly under her arm. I felt sorry for her and didn't know what to do.

Finally, I said, "Esther, let me see the flag." Reluctantly, very reluctantly, she handed it to me while the kids cowered behind their grandmother, their brown eyes as big as frisbees. Their mother, the weaver's daughter, said she had to use the restroom.

Cautiously, I unwrapped the flag. It was odd, to say the least. My son, who had been watching, smiled and left the room. The Texas flag was perfect in every detail except one, the lone star. It was all out of proportion and lay on its side in an ungainly manner. Esther was bawling out loud by now.

I smiled and said, "Well, that is a funny looking star, but I like it." Esther was afraid that I wouldn't pay her the promised four hundred dollars, and she knew no other trader who would want to buy it. I assured her that the flag was okay. Everything was fine. The kids relaxed and raced around the showroom, we all had a Pepsi, and Esther took the money, plus a few dollars for gas and food, and left for home.

My son came into the showroom and said, "I almost laughed out loud. The star looks like a KOA campground sign that got knocked on its ass by a truck." It really did. Today I still have the Texas flag. It is not for sale at any price. I can't sell memories like that, and my Texas flag experience is a fine memory.

During the Pepsi years, I spent many hours with traders talking about weaving, witchcraft, business, families, and so on. With frequent visits I developed some close personal relationships. They were not just customers, they were true friends. Ed Foutz, who owned Shiprock Trading Company, gave me a small Santa Claus pictorial just before Christmas one year. We had traded rugs and soda pop for many moons. He wanted to thank me for some special favor. I loved the little bright green and red Santa.

Years later I thought that it would be fun to have a pictorial with a Christmas tree and a greeting, "Happy New Year 1980." I ordered it from the weaver in the summer of 1979. The rug arrived after Easter, 1981. Another time, I ordered a pumpkin rug for Halloween. It arrived between Christmas and New Year's day. Not all special orders turn out like this. I have ordered flags, banners, greetings, and many others, and the majority are fine. When an error occurs I think it adds to the charm. At least it is good for a smile.

I often hear potential buyers say that pictorials are new to Navajo weaving and that they like more "traditional" weavings. I point out to them that birds, animals, trains, and other common objects were woven into rugs and blankets back in the 1800s. When the railroad pushed westward across Navajoland, many rugs were woven featuring a steam locomotive pulling passenger cars across the desert. I have several pictorials, one with a warrior on horseback, that date to the early twentieth century. I once bought a large pictorial woven at Ganado in 1921. It is full of birds, animals, bows, arrows, and other symbols.

Asuna Blackhorse is nearly ninety-six years old. During the 1960s I used to buy her finely woven pictorials. She specialized in weaving the art work of famed Pueblo artist Pablita Velarde. The last time I stopped to see Asuna she told me she had lost her eye-sight. She could see only the bare outline of objects and couldn't weave. Then, unexpectedly, she showed up with a rug. It was rough and uneven, totally different from her early works, yet simple and straightforward. It was the footprints of a man, a boy, and a dog. My son and daughter gave it to me as a gift. Just looking at it brings a ray of sunshine into any day. Asuna saw the footprints of her son, grandson, and their dog in the sand or snow and thought, "I can do that, even if I'm almost blind."

Navajo pictorial weaving is a thriving art form. Weavers let their imaginations run, and the results are sometimes like something Grandma Moses might have created. Recently a weaver wove a rug depicting the loading of animals onto Noah's ark. One by one the animals file up the gangplank as a Navajo-looking Noah looks on. The same weaver captured the mood of the Navajo Tribal Fair in a pictorial complete with a ferris wheel, sno-cone stands, and pop-corn vendors.

In my opinion the finest pictorial weavers are Isabel John and her daughter-in-law Geanita John. These two ladies live in Navajoland not far from Canyon de Chelly, Arizona. Hand-spun, hand-dyed yarn predominates in their weavings. The pieces range in size from eighteen by twenty-four inches to heroic sizes of eight to ten feet in length. Isabel was the featured weaver when the Museum of Inter-national Folk Art in Santa Fe opened the new Girard Wing. Sothe-by's in New York used a photo of a large pictorial by Isabel on the cover of an auction catalog, and the Denver Art Museum displays one of her large pictorials in the Native American Wing. A large Isabel John is in the acclaimed "Lost and Found Traditions" exhibit that has toured the country. Geanita John's peaceful pictorial of a Navajo fam-ily scene is an important weaving in the Durango Collection.

Geanita and Isabel are traditional Navajo women, proud of their skill, creative ability, and Navajo culture. Navajo is the language spoken in their homes. It's a happy family filled with love and un-derstanding. Two remarkably talented weavers, working together, point the way for a whole new generation of Navajo women who wish to continue the tradition of weaving. A weaver does not have to be bound by strict artistic guidelines, thus pictorial weavers are imaginative, creative artists in the fullest sense. Isabel and

Navajo rancher encounters moon lander: "Hey, what are you guys doin' out there?"

Geanita's pictorials impart a sense of peace and well being in homes and offices here and abroad, bringing a true American folk art into people's lives.

Today, somewhere in Navajoland, pictorial weavers are preparing their looms for weaving. Long-dead grandmothers are consulted. Images form in the weaver's mind and colors are chosen. The wool is carded, spun, and dyed, and nimble fingers thread wool weft through wool warp. The rug slowly begins to take shape while the theme unfolds. Children watch and daughters comment. It is the time of testing for the weaver. All of her creative energy is focused on making the detail of the pictorial come to life as a carefully crafted work of art or a whimsical piece.

Once in a while a weaver will ask for a suggestion from me regarding her next subject. I sometimes get bored with repetitious designs: too many cows, too many sheep, and the same mountains in the background. Recently a weaver told me, with a twinkle in her eye, "I've got a good idea. I want to make a rocket ship. You know that thing those guys landed on the moon. I really didn't believe that happened because nobody supposed to go to the moon. I want to do a rug with that thing on the moon, in a field of moon grass with the sheep grazing around it and a hogan in the distance and a Navajo with a big tall hat looking up at that spaceship. What do you think?"

What do I think? I can hardly wait.

The Durango Collection

Mark Winter had a dream. He wanted to assemble a few Navajo blankets into a modest collection that could be exhibited around the country in museums, schools, and Indian art shows. That was 1976. Mark and I had been partners in his old Navajo rug business since 1975. The partnership started in an off-hand manner, no formal papers, no big deal, just a handshake. It grew far beyond our wildest dreams.

I met Mark when he came into my office in the Pepsi building in Durango. He asked if he could take some of our older Navajo rugs on consignment for a few days. He said he lived in Pagosa Springs, Colorado, about sixty-five miles from Durango.

"I have a customer coming from California who might be interested in several of your rugs. I'll either have the rugs back here by Tuesday or have the money in your hands by then."

It sounded fair. He was a nice-looking guy with a little of the '60s still in him. I liked him and his wife Barbara right off the bat. On Tuesday Mark came in with cash in hand. Mark departed with another stack of our rugs. Several days later he came back with the money, and a suggestion.

"I think that we should buy a few good weavings as a nucleus for a collection. I'm thinking that if we had a Chief's blanket, a serape, and maybe a Moki and a Germantown I could display them at the shows I attend. It would be an educational, hands-on project, and will probably bring in a lot of business."

He was enthusiastic. "I'm sure that we can have a really representative collection with only a few pieces. I don't want it to get too involved."

That was the start. When we sold the majority interest to Richard and Mary Lyn Ballantine in 1989, the Durango Collection had developed into one of the finest private collections of textiles in the country. We had over two hundred pieces in the active collection and it was still growing.

Mark sincerely believed that most of the fine Southwestern textiles were locked in museum vaults, available only to scholars and not to the general public. He stated simply, "I want to show people who are interested in the Navajo and interested in weaving a few very fine pieces. I want them to be able to get up close, to be able to touch and feel them and transfer some of the energy and mystique from the blankets to the person. We can generate a lot of sales for our business if we can educate people as we go along."

It all sounded fine to me. We agreed that we should limit the amount of money we put in the unnamed collection to ten thousand dollars.

"No problem," Mark assured me. We already had a considerable investment in inventory for sale in his business, and I knew that we could probably float a small loan if necessary.

We agreed to start looking for our first acquisition. Less than a week later, a Bayeta Chief's blanket came up for sale from a friend of ours who was a dealer in Pittsburgh. Mark flew back to inspect the blanket, but when he reported back to me I was shocked.

"Jackson, this is an important piece, but it's in need of some repair. It has one big hole right near the center that you could throw a bobcat through, and the edges need some work. It's beautiful! Apparently a man bought it for fifteen dollars at a garage sale and then discovered what he had. He sold it to Pat (our dealer friend) for a thousand, and she wants fifteen hundred. I think it is a good buy."

Horrified, I swallowed hard and said okay. I was even more horrified when we found that the restoration, according to an estimate by Albert Ouzunian's Persian Rug Company, would bring our investment to over five thousand dollars. That was half of what we had agreed on for the entire collection.

After several months under Ouzunian's care, the restoration was complete and Mark brought the blanket back to Durango. It was truly lovely, and I agreed that it was worth the money, and much more. It was dazzling. Mark modeled it in the showroom for all of us to see. It shimmered in the light; the diamonds on the corners and in the center of the nine-point blanket seemed to leap out from the textile and suspend themselves in air. It was mesmerizing.

Enthusiasm for the idea of having a fine collection began to dominate our thoughts. Mark worked hard to build his business, while keeping an eye out for good pieces.

I cautioned him, "Mark, let's just take this one step at a time. Let's take it one blanket at a time and see where we are. We are going to have to be careful or we'll get in over our heads financially."

Mark agreed. "I think that I can continue to buy for the business and buy for the collection, so we can start trading up for other pieces. Everything we buy is money in the bank."

That wasn't true at all. There was no money in the bank. This was brought home to me by Nick Turner, my good friend who owned the Bank of Durango.

Nick was angry. "What the hell is going on with Mark Winter and you? We have an overdraft up here that would choke a mule. It needs attending to right now. Today. Are you sure you know what you're doing with that Winter fellow?"

Mark was on his way back from California with a new blanket for the collection. He had described it over the phone as being a possible "Slave Blanket," one that had been woven on a Navajo loom by a Navajo slave in a Spanish hacienda. He had found it on a table at a gun show and snatched it up moments before another dealer spotted it. Just days before he had found a Moki serape, a banded, somber, and elegant piece with natural brown wool and rich, deep blue indigo. Mark felt the Moki and the Slave blankets "filled a gap" in the collection. I told him the gap that needed filling had a dollar sign in front of it. He had had good sales, but had reinvested all the proceeds in inventory, the Moki and the Slave Blanket. The bank account was in sad shape, and I had no money to put into the business.

Mark and I went to the Bank of Durango as soon as he got back to Colorado. Turner was waiting. Two more overdrafts had just hit the bank. He greeted us coolly, and then got down to business.

"We can't let this go on any longer. These overdrafts must be covered and I mean today."

I explained our goals for the collection. Mark showed Turner some photos of the few items in the collection and a detailed explanation of our costs and what he considered a conservative market value for each textile. I suggested that we might put on a show at the Bank of Durango featuring the rugs from the collection.

"What we really need is a long-term line of credit so we will have the finances to buy something spectacular when we find it. You know, to fill in the gaps. We'll pledge the entire collection as collateral."

Nick smiled and said, "If we are going to finance this for you fellows, how about calling it 'The Bank of Durango Collection'?"

At that moment I would have called it anything he had in mind if he'd let us off the hook. I don't think Mark ever realized how close we were to losing the whole collection. Mark is a sharp buyer and a shrewd trader. Once Turner understood that we weren't collecting old saddle blankets and worn-out rugs he came up with an arrangement for financing the collection. The whole thing hadn't taken thirty minutes. It was a fairly complicated deal and quite expensive. Interest rates in the late '70s were nearly twenty percent. I was delighted. We all shook hands when Mark had a suggestion: "Why don't we call it 'The Durango Collection'?"

The three of us agreed that we would exhibit the collection for the premiere showing in the lobby of the Bank of Durango. The building had been remodeled several years before in Santa Fe style. The ceilings were high, the walls were painted an off-white and the lighting was wonderful. A *portal* over the sidewalk in the front of the bank sheltered anything in the building from the direct rays of the sun.

In the summer of 1978 we installed the Durango Collection at the bank in preparation for a month-long showing. Nick Turner and the bank hosted a reception on a Friday night. The reaction from locals who came to see "some old Navajo rugs" was overwhelmingly favorable. Durangoans had long owned Navajo rugs, but few had ever seen the wonders of Bayeta serapes, Chief's blankets, two-hundred-year-old Saltillo blankets, and dazzling Germantowns. Each piece was properly labeled and arranged in such a manner that vistors did not interfere with bank business. To beef up the collection we borrowed several pieces from other collectors and Dr. Robert Delaney, Director of the Center for Southwest Studies at Fort Lewis College.

After the show and the favorable comments, Nick eased our financial strain by buying a nice group of rugs for permanent display in the bank. He said, "Now, we really have a Bank of Durango Collection."

Displaying the collection in the bank was a good move, but to gain the real exposure we needed a museum show. We contacted my good friend Donald Hague, Director of the Utah Museum of Natural History, who agreed to host a show. In October of 1980 the Durango Collection opened for a month-long exhibit.

Immediately after the Utah show, in cooperation with Noel Bennett's "Shared Horizons," a seminar on Navajo weaving, we set up the collection at the Wheelwright Museum in Santa Fe.

Mark continued to collect. "We need to fill in a few gaps," he'd say. Nick Turner was supportive and we were paying the bank on a regular basis. It wasn't easy because of Mark's unpredictable need for cash whenever he found that special piece to "fill the gap."

Our big break came when Joyce Herrold, curator at the Denver Museum of Natural History, agreed to host the collection during the summer of 1985. As a promotional tool, the museum produced an outstanding video for us. Much of it was taped on the Navajo Reservation where we were able to feature interviews with contemporary weavers. Following Denver, Mark and I had several smaller museum shows. The Sierra Nevada Museum of Art in Reno displayed the collection for two months. Then we moved on to various other museums, galleries, and colleges. We were both busy lecturing on the collection for most of the time between 1984 and 1987.

I have often said that Mark attracts good textiles like a lightning rod attacts lightning. Sometimes from out of nowhere we'd get a call informing us that a blanket was for sale. If it was a significant piece, one we thought would fill that famous gap in the collection, we'd buy it and perhaps sell another piece to pay for it. It was a constant upgrading of material. From the beginning, we had agreed that we'd have only the best. We bought nothing but the finest available at the time. Mark was excellent at it. He knew what he wanted and when he found something unusual we'd talk it over, make the arrangement on the loan, and buy it.

Those years were some of the most challenging in my life. My experience had been mostly with contemporary rugs. The fine antique pieces boggled my mind. Mark began to be a celebrity in the antique Indian artifact business. Sometimes I wished he had remained that rather naïve young man he was when we first met, but Mark handled his success well.

The one person who helped us most during the time we were assembling the Durango Collection was Dr. Joe Ben Wheat of the University of Colorado Museum. Joe is a renowned archaeologist and historian who writes extensively on the Southwest. At this writing he is at work on a definitive treatment of Navajo weaving. No matter how busy Joe was or how hectic his schedule, he never failed to take the time to look at a new textile, discuss it with us, and give us his opinion.

I remember the time we located a fragment of a Navajo two-piece dress from a private collection. It had come into the possession of a trader I knew. Bill Bobb of Santa Fe, who was working for Toh-Atin at the time, saw it and told me about it. I mentioned it to Mark, who was on his way through Durango to a show in Los Angeles. Mark stopped in to see the piece and called me immediately.

"Jackson, if we can buy it, that could be the single most important piece in the Durango Collection. I think that it could date back to 1750. Drive down there and see if we can borrow it to take to Dr. Wheat."

I agreed to go but told Mark that I would not be able to leave until the following day. Mark called the same day shortly before noon. He called again from Mexican Water in midafternoon, and from Kayenta, then Flagstaff. Finally, at midnight he called from Needles, California.

"Jackson, listen to me. Please go down there first thing in the morning. This is important."

I'd gotten the message long before that.

I slept little that night and arose early to drive to New Mexico. I

arranged to borrow the textile and flew to Denver with it the following morning, arriving at Joe and Pat Wheat's house in Boulder
shortly before noon.

Joe greeted me. "Mark says you have something special to show
me."

I took the tattered, patched, forlorn textile from my suitcase and
spread it out in front of Joe. I thought the pipe might fall from his
mouth.

"This is the rarest of all Navajo textiles. I'd date this to the mid-
1700s."

We pored over it for a long time, examining every detail. It had
been pieced together from two separate dresses. Two centuries ago,
a Navajo woman had worn it for many years before finally discard-
ing it.

Strangely, there was something unholy about the piece. When I
returned from Boulder that evening I took it home and spread it out
in the living room to show to my wife. My old dog, Herbie, roused
from a sound sleep, moseyed over to take a sniff. One was enough.
He took off out the front door, crawled under the fence, and
headed down the road. He was out of there and didn't return for
several days. I have often wondered if the old dog sensed something
that we didn't. Perhaps the original owner of the dress was murdered or met with some tragedy. A *chindi*, or spirit, inhabited the
dress, I'm sure. I took it to the Pepsi plant that very night and
stored it in the vault. Two of the office workers complained that the
vault was cold and clammy—as if a cloud hung over everything.
Only after we began displaying the dress in a special case at various
museums did this sensation dissipate.

Weavings were being added to the collection at a phenomenal
rate. It seems that hardly a week passed without a new and exciting
addition. As an example, Mark bought a group of early twentieth-
century blankets from Sotheby's in New York. They came from the
estate of the late Chee Dodge, the first tribal chairman of the Navajo Nation. When Mark returned from a trip with a new acquisition he often stopped off at Toh-Atin. Jackson, my son, and frequently Antonia, my daughter, would join Mark and me as we sat
on the floor admiring the new textile. These moments were some of
the most rewarding of the entire time that I worked with Mark.

Sometimes we'd all sit in silence for several minutes contemplating the piece. I can recall many times that each of us reached out to stroke the newly arrived piece as if to assure it that it had found a good home.

All of us were aware that fine blankets and serapes didn't materialize from thin air. A weaver, a human being, living in primitive conditions had spent weeks and maybe months working on what we considered a masterpiece. We tried to put a personality to each textile in the collection.

When we had the chance to welcome a new piece we often found fascinating weaving variations such as a change of yarn, a misplaced weft, different colored warps, or a subtle piece of contrasting color woven into a plain background. We would try to attach in our own minds the long departed weaver to her blanket. All we could do was speculate. It is sad that weavers were never identified, or if they were, their identity has been lost. The textiles, in many collections, have become more important than the long-forgotten weaver. We did what we could to honor her and not merely the textile.

Through most of the 1980s we continued to add, upgrade, and expand the collection. Finally, it grew beyond our means, and we decided to sell. By then we had also added a group of contemporary Navajo weavings to document the continuity of the tradition from the mid-1700s to the present. Several foreign museums, including one in Germany, were interested. Fortunately the Ballantines decided to buy it and to retain Mark as a partner and curator. It felt good to know that the Durango Collection would remain in Durango.

The Ballantines and Mark have expanded the collection with a great variety of textiles that Mark and I could only dream of. The collection continues to grow as the famous "gaps" are filled in. It was always intended as a living collection, constantly changing with new textiles from Mexico, South America, and New Mexico intermingled with the familiar Navajo classic blankets.

Whenever it is on display I try to go to view it. Most of the pieces have personal memories for me, but when I see the original Third Phase Chief blanket that started the whole thing I get goose bumps. It is vibrant, more appealing, and more intriguing than it was when we first found it. I wonder if that fellow who bought it at a garage sale in Pittsburgh has any idea what he started.

Trading with Santiago

Like Father Liebler, Santiago Moquino also came into Jackson Hardware on a frigid February night in 1946. He made his way to the office at the rear of the store. I watched him closely as he walked down the long display aisle toward the office. Not that I could avoid doing so: he locked his sharp, dark eyes on mine as soon as he saw me. A short, stocky, older man with a bull neck, he seemed to waddle as he walked.

I knew he was a Pueblo Indian from the Rio Grande Valley, but I wondered what he was doing in Durango in midwinter. He looked like a Santo Domingo but I couldn't tell for sure. Domingos and other Pueblo Indians who sold jewelry and other Indian items usually avoided Durango during the winter when the tourist business slumped, and Durango was not much of a tourist town in those days—even in summer.

He was wrapped in a well-worn Pendleton blanket, a red bandana around his head, with his long hair tied in a knot. He wore turquoise earrings and good silver bracelets. Several fine strings of coral and turquoise beads hung from his neck. I guessed he might be in his late 60s. The light jacket under his blanket offered little protection against the cold. The temperature had stayed below freezing all day.

I greeted him. "Hi there. Pretty cold out there, isn't it? What can I do for you?"

"You wanna buy some jewelry?"

"No, we don't carry jewelry. You better hurry to one of the jewelry stores in town. They'll be closing about now."

He gave me a knowing look. "I went dere already. They don't want nothin'. How about tradin' for some hardware stuff."

"Where are you from?" I asked him.

"Santo Domingo. You know where dat is?"

"Sure, it's between Albuquerque and Santa Fe, down on the Rio Grande. I've been there lots of times with my parents. I guessed you were from Santo Domingo when you walked in the store. What are you doing up here this time of the year?"

"I'm sellin' jewelry. I need money to get my tractor fixed."

"You have some nice looking turquoise. What's your name?"

"Santiago. Santiago Moquino."

"Well, Santiago, I'm Jackson. This is no time to sell jewelry in Durango. The tourists are gone, and everyone spent too much money on Christmas. My dad used to say you Domingos would go to the gates of hell to sell jewelry. Durango is just about as bad this time of the year."

"You wanna trade, Jack?"

"The name is Jackson, not Jack."

"I'm gonna call you Jack. Jackson sound funny. You got lotta files, axes, hammers, and tools. I got lotta jewelry. You give me some tools, and I'll give you jewelry. I can sell the tools back home. You can sell the jewelry. Lotta people gonna come in and buy jewelry."

He continued to probe me with his dark eyes. I sized him up as a sharp trader. He was here to make a trade and not deal in excuses.

"Come on. Let's trade. I gotta meet my boy at the Penny store and start back to Albuquerque before it snows."

Against my better judgment, I agreed to look at what he had. The jewelry was in two leather pouches slung over his shoulders like bandoliers. I noticed his concha belt only after he had loosened the Pendleton blanket. It was old, made of heavy silver, with a nice turquoise stone in each concha.

"I'll trade you tools for your concha belt."

"No!" His eyes blazed. "Dat's my belt. It's not for sale. This other stuff is what I have to trade."

He emptied the contents of his pouch on the showcase. Most of the jewelry was the old-fashioned Santo Domingo chip-inlay type made of melted wax phonograph records, bits of treated turquoise and coral. It didn't appeal to me. Years later this crude jewelry would be a highly prized item. That evening in 1946 I didn't want any of it.

"You look the jewelry over, Jack, and I'll get some tools together." I liked his confidence. He knew that "no" was not an acceptable answer. He may have waddled but he had the determination of a bulldog.

Closing time came. I told the store clerks that I'd stay and work with Santiago. I was enjoying myself more than anytime since returning from the army. Two hours later Santiago left the store with a box full of tools, and I had a meager selection of Santo Domingo jewelry. I got the short end of the proverbial stick, but it had been fun.

I decided not to tell my mother about the trade until she had finished some work on my father's estate. I put the jewelry in a paper sack and stashed it in the safe. I wasn't too proud of my trading skills anyway.

A few weeks later she found it in the safe. "Jackson, do you know about this? What's this stuff?"

I told her the whole story and she laughed. "Your dad would have gotten a kick out of that. You may end up turning this store into a trading post. Why don't we just keep it and give it away to customers as presents? We can't sell tourists things like that."

I put it in the locked display case with the pocket knives so we might keep track of it. To my surprise we started selling it. People actually liked it and wanted to buy more. Customers came in to see the unique Santo Domingo jewelry. Soon we had sold almost the entire lot and made a small profit. There was one problem: we didn't know how to get in touch with Santiago to replenish our stock.

Several months later Santiago returned. He showed up in Durango to sell to the few tourists who came to town in those days. I was delighted to see him. We spent most of one afternoon trading jewelry for axes, hammers, saws, and knives. The old man was a sharp trader and would have been right at home in a Middle East-ern bazaar. Santo Domingos have always had the reputation as the Lebanese traders of the Southwest.

From 1946 until 1957 Santiago and I traded several times each year. One time he wanted a refrigerator and a washing machine. Electric power had come to Santo Domingo. That's where I had to draw the line. In May of 1957 we sold the hardware store, and I be-came sales manager at Pepsi. I didn't see Santiago for several months. Then, early one summer morning, I met him on Main Avenue.

"Jack! Where you been? I been in dat store and dey don't want no jewelry. Where you workin'?"

"Santiago, I work at the Pepsi plant down in the next block. Come down and see me, and I'll give you a case of Pepsi."

That afternoon Santiago came to the Pepsi plant. He was disap-pointed because the new hardware store owners didn't want to trade. Santiago and I went down into my small basement office to talk and drink a Pepsi. A few weeks earlier I had begun trading Pepsi for Navajo rugs on the reservation.

Santiago noticed some of the rugs on a chair in my office. I asked him, "Do you want to trade some jewelry for a few rugs? I think I could sell the jewelry to some of our customers and employees."

"You got Navajo rugs, Jack. I need Navajo rugs. I sell lotta Na-vajo rugs. You got any more?"

"Well, we don't have a safe place down here so I keep most of them up at the house. Let's go up there and we'll look."

At my home we piled rugs in one stack and jewelry in another. He wanted more rugs than I could afford to give. At one point he got mad about it.

"How come you won't give me what I want?"

"Because I can't sell all that Santo Domingo jewelry. I tell you what I'll do, Santiago, you trade me your concha belt, and you can have those rugs."

He snapped back at me, "No! My belt's not for sale. Gimme those two rugs, and you can have the bunch of earrings."

"Okay, Santiago, but if you ever sell that belt, sell it to me."

Santiago and I traded rugs for jewelry for many years. I remem-ber one time when he came to the office (we had moved the rugs to the Pepsi-Cola building) and, as always, we started piling up rugs and jewelry and picking the items we wanted.

But on this day he was aggressive.

"You been takin' me, Jack. I can't sell dose rugs for dose prices you got on dem. I gotta get more rugs for the jewelry."

"Santiago, I'm being fair with you. I have a file drawer full of your jewelry that I can't sell. My partners are raising hell about our trades."

We squatted on the floor with a pile of rugs and jewelry. I spotted an extraordinary turquoise necklace and reached to put it in my pile.

"No! Put it back!" Santiago said. He reached across the rugs and slapped my hand. When he reached for a rug, I did the same thing to him. We had a royal hand slapping contest. We laughed and swore and tried to be angry with each other, but it was simply too much fun. We were testing each other, and we both knew it. But we weren't getting much trading done. Finally, he got tired and walked out. I knew he'd be back.

About midafternoon he returned.

"Jack, we gotta talk this over. I need rugs and you need jewelry. You buy me a cuppa coffee so we can talk."

Within fifteen minutes Santiago had the rugs he needed and I had my usual pile of earrings and necklaces. The turquoise beads I wanted were not included in the trade. Santiago made an excuse about not being able to trade the piece.

"Next time I come, Jack, I'll bring a better one."

That evening I saw Santiago in the newly opened Diamond Belle Saloon in Durango's Strater Hotel. The place was packed. A honky-tonk piano tinkled away, happy drinkers sang, drank, and toasted each other. I spotted Santiago in the balcony, just above the gold-leaf sign that proclaimed, "Work is the Curse of the Drinking Class."

Santiago was talking to Nancy Elliot, a friend of mine, and two other people. He saw me but didn't wave. Nancy recognized me in the crowd and motioned for me to come up to the balcony. I edged my way through the crowded bar, up the stairway, and finally reached her table. Santiago looked at me without blinking an eye.

Nancy greeted me. "Hi, Jackson, these are friends of mine from the East. They want to buy this rug from this man. I saw you down there and said you might be able to advise them."

"Sure. I'll be glad to help. What did he tell you about the rug? Did he say he wove it?"

"No, he said that he traded jewelry for it. He said the rug was from a different tribe."

"Do you like the rug?"

"Oh, yes. We don't want to pay too much. Is a hundred dollars fair?"

I looked at Santiago. His eyes were on me. Neither of us blinked. I'll bet he was one hell of a poker player.

"Well, if you like the rug, the price is okay. It isn't a really fine rug, but look at this old man. Look at his face. He must be eighty years old. Look at his clothes; look at his jewelry. You will be able to tell your kids and grandkids that you bought this rug from a real Indian. You'll treasure it forever."

I went back to my table and watched Santiago close the deal. Santiago got the money; the visitors got the rug. Everyone was pleased.

Santiago came down the stairs and passed by my table. He whispered in my ear, "You good man, Jack. I'm gonna buy you a beer." He patted me on the shoulder, smiled, and walked over to the bartender to order me a beer. Then he disappeared into the summer night.

I didn't see him again until October, when I made a trip to the Santo Domingo Pueblo. I had popped in and out of Santo Domingo on frequent trips during the past few years, but I had never been to Santiago's home. That day, I took time to really look at the pueblo and to absorb the sights, smells, and sounds of the ancient place. I imagined that it looked much as it had when the Spanish first saw it in the sixteenth century—a village of one-story adobe dwellings arranged on streets and plazas, each building built directly against its neighbor. Small children played in the streets, and old men soaked up the warm autumn sun oblivious to my slowly moving car. A few junk cars with flat tires littered the yards. Fresh red chilé hung in long *ristras* from the exposed *vigas*, or beams, on each home, drying slowly in the autumn sun. The entire village lay under a blanket of dust. There were few trees.

I asked a woman who ran a small store near the main plaza for the location of the Moquino home.

"Oh! You must mean Santiago, that Moquino who is always sellin' jewelry. He lives down the road toward the river, right alongside the railroad tracks. It's on the right-hand side, about a mile from here. He got lotta trees by his house. There's a bunch of old cars and a tractor in the yard."

I found the place without trouble. In the yard I saw Santiago's tractor. I felt as if I had found an old friend. Santiago came out to greet me.

"What you doin' down here, Jack? You bring me some Navajo rugs and some soda pop?"

"I just stopped by to see you and to meet your tractor. I brought you a case of Pepsi."

He laughed and asked me in for a bowl of green chilé and some fresh bread and strong coffee. I looked around the modest home and marveled at the rugs, pottery, and beadwork. I met his wife, a frail lady, who had been in poor health for some time. She laughed when Santiago told her of our trading encounters. They spoke to each other entirely in the Keres language. Santiago spoke some English and was fluent in Spanish. However, he preferred to speak his native tongue whenever possible.

I loved to talk and joke with him about his customs and his lifestyle. In return he always kidded me about the "white man's" ways.

"Santiago, I want to ask you about your language. I know you speak good Spanish, but your English is not too good. But when you talk to your family and friends you use your funny old Keres language."

I watched for his reaction. There was none; only silence. I continued.

"Santiago, your kids don't speak Spanish very well, but they speak good English. Tell me about that."

"Well, Jack, when I was a young man, alla people in New Mexico speak Spanish. To get a job or sell jewelry alla Indians had to speak Spanish. Now alla people speak English, and my kids have to speak English to get a job or sell jewelry."

"I know that, Santiago, but why do you still speak that funny old Indian language?"

This was a real jab. He looked at me for a few moments, then with a twinkle in his eye, he said, "Well, Jack, you think you guys gonna be here forever?"

It was just like when we traded and he got the best deal. Now he had had the last word. Just before I got in the car he asked if I would like a *ristra* of red chilé.

"Of course. That's very nice of you, Santiago."

"Well, I make you a good deal, Jack. Only fifteen dollars."

I had bought a longer string for twelve in Espanola only a few hours earlier. Santiago had struck again. I laughed at myself as I drove out of his yard. Golly, I liked that old man. He could be infuriatingly stubborn, even downright selfish, but I always hated to say adios to him.

My wife and I decided we would like to have a portrait of Santiago. The next time he came to Durango we talked about it.

"Santiago, we would like to have a portrait painted of you. We know a fine artist here in Durango. You met her, Mrs. Healy. She said that she would love to have you sit for her."

"What's a portrait, Jack?"

"It's a painting of a person. This will be a painting of you, in color."

"Well, Jack, I never had my pitcher painted. I guess it would be all right. How much you gonna pay me?" Santiago never changed. Money was always first.

"Well, how much do you think it will be worth? It will probably take several hours."

"I'll see how much I think it is worth after the pitcher is painted."

He agreed to return the following Saturday. He always drove up with his son or some friend from Santo Domingo, but this time he took the bus. He said that he would stay at the Strater Hotel. "Dat guy Earl, the owner, he give me a good price."

Isabel John spinning yarn, 1989. (Keith Jay)

Weaver-image pictorial. (Keith Jay)

"That black thing is a pile of coal."

Happy New Year, 1980. (Bruce Conrad)

Santa Claus pictorial. (Bruce Conrad)

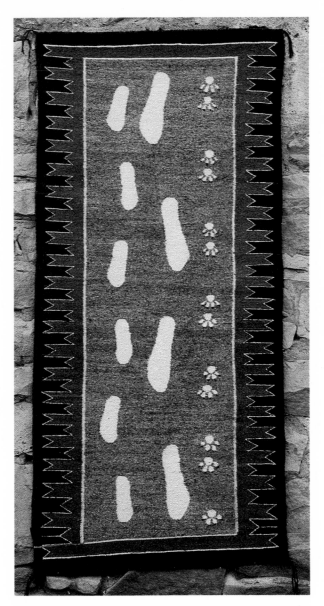

A man, a boy, and a dog. Asuna Blackhorse, 1987.
(Bruce Conrad)

Third Phase Bayeta Chief's blanket, Durango Collection.

Navajo serape. "Mark snatched it off a display at a gun show."

Santiago Moquino, by Martha Healy.

Early on Saturday I went to the hotel to pick up Santiago and take him for his sitting. He was waiting for me in front all decked out in a new shirt, new bandana, and a wonderful string of beads. He was a sight straight out of the 1920s Fred Harvey Indian Detour brochure. Earl Barker, the hotel owner, was talking to Santiago.

"You know this fellow, Jackson?"

"I surely do, Earl. Santiago and I have been doing business for a long time."

Earl tried to frown but couldn't help smiling. "He is the sharpest trader I have ever seen, a regular skinflint. Last night he needed a room and he asked how much. I told him ten dollars. He said two. I said seven and he said two. We finally settled for two-fifty. Then he wanted me to throw in breakfast!"

Santiago laughed and said that next time he'd bargain for a dollar-fifty.

When we arrived at the Healy home, another local artist, Lenore Hamilton, decided she would like to paint him too. I didn't know how this would go over with Santiago.

"Do I have to stay twice as long? Can they do it at the same time?" I assured him that they could.

I left him with the two artists and didn't see him until Marty Healy dropped him off at my office late in the afternoon.

"Boy, Jack, dat's hard work. I been sittin' since morning. I got tired and tried to take a nap, but dose ladies say, 'Santiago, wake up! You can't go to sleep now. Wake up, Santiago!' I want two hundred dollars for dat work. You take me to the bus station?

"I'm gonna come back next week and see how the pitcher looks," he told me as he boarded the bus for Albuquerque.

The next Saturday Santiago returned to Durango, boiling mad.

"What dose ladies gonna do with my pitcher? They gonna sell it? Jack, dose Indians just raise hell with me. They say, 'Santiago, you sold your soul. You gonna die. You sold your soul. You gonna live forever in that pitcher. Why you do dat Santiago?' "

His words cut me like a knife. I would not do anything to offend him. He and I were too close. I assured him that my family would get one painting and the other would be a gift to Mrs. Healy's husband. Nothing would be sold. We went to see both artists to talk about his fears and what the Indians told him. Reluctantly,

Santiago agreed with me. He really seemed proud of the portraits. He admired them for several minutes.

"What do you think now, Santiago? You are a handsome guy!"

"All right, Jack. I'll go back and tell those Indians it's okay. Now, you wanna buy some jewelry?"

The next time I saw Santiago, it was early on a Sunday morning, just before Christmas. He was selling jewelry on the steps of the Strater Hotel. He called out to me, "Jack, what you gonna do today?"

"We are going up in the mountains and get a Christmas tree."

"Jack, I'm eighty-six years old. I never got a Christmas tree."

"Well, you come with us. We are going up to Electra Lake. The snow will be deep, and it will be cold, so wear a warm coat."

We spent the afternoon tramping through foot-deep snow searching for the right tree. We finally found a fine Colorado blue spruce, cut it, and dragged it through the snow to the car, lashing it securely on the ski rack.

"We're going to go home and decorate it, Santiago. Come up and help."

Santiago had a marvelous time. We played Christmas music. Santiago joined in the singing. He seemed to be full of the Christmas spirit when I took him back to the Strater Hotel.

The next day he came to the office to talk. "Jack, I need money to fix my tractor. You lend me six hundred dollars and I leave my belt with you. If anything happens to me, you keep the belt. Don't give it to my boys. They will just sell it."

I gave him the money and put the belt in the safe where it would be when he wanted it. He touched the belt one last time and walked out the door.

That was the last time I saw him. We heard from one of the traveling Santo Domingos that he had died later that winter. At first it was a terrible shock. I couldn't understand why his son hadn't called me so my family could go to the funeral mass at the church in Santo Domingo. I really loved that old man. We had been doing business for over twenty years, and I didn't even know of his death until much later. Several months later his son came in to ask about the belt. I thought of Santiago and our last meeting. I said that I had it in safe keeping and would keep it. I knew Santiago wanted me to have it.

Santiago's belt.

I look back on my friendship with Santiago Moquino and recall our trading days. He was one of the last and one of the best old-time traveling Santo Domingo traders. Today there are many younger Domingos on the road, and the Santo Domingo jewelry tradition continues. Santo Domingo looks much as it did many years ago, though the Pueblo is doing well now: the homes are well kept, nice cars are on every plaza, and the young people go to colleges and universities. Junk cars still litter the streets, but prosperity is evident. Yet despite all outside influence, Santo Domingo continues to be the most conservative of all the Pueblos in its customs and ceremonies. Several hundred tribal members dance in the frequent ceremonies such as the summer corn dance. No cameras are allowed, and visitors mind their manners. Sometimes, without explanation, the Pueblo suddenly closes to all outsiders. For me, it is always an interesting place to visit, but it just isn't the same without that old man. I catch myself looking for him in the crowd during the dances.

His spirit probably looks in on his belt once in a while. Once or twice a year, for special occasions, I take it out of the safe-deposit box, polish it, and wear it. Someone almost always tries to buy it. I'm sure Santiago would be proud when I say, "This is a special belt and it's not for sale. A dear friend of mine asked me to keep it for him and that's what I am doing. You never know when he is going to pop in and want it."

Search for a Dead Soldier

I looked at my watch, 3:00 P.M. on a blistering June day, 1988. The temperature knocked ninety-five degrees. My feet hurt, my back ached, and my mouth felt like I'd been chewing sand. The sun-soaked canyon walls concentrated the fierce heat like an oven. The few scraggly trees gave little shade.

I said to my companion, Joe Ben Wheat, "I wonder what the hell we're doing out here, Joe? This sun is really bad."

Joe smiled. "You're the guy who told me about the mysterious dead soldier. I'm just following you!"

We had walked for three hours on what was to be a short hike into a narrow, winding canyon. Time had slipped away. We had no water, no food, no candy, just cameras, binoculars, and a map. We had taken off totally unprepared. Our lunch, along with water, cold beer, and sunscreen, was locked back in Joe's car. According to the map we had walked more than three miles—a long three miles.

When we started out we scrambled down a steep rock and dirt face from a sandstone bench alongside the canyon. We slid in a trouser-tearing, butt-blistering, get-out-of-the-way slide to the canyon floor. We then walked up the dry creekbed through soft sand. The vermillion walls got higher and higher as we moved into the canyon. Our plan had been to go a short distance "to take a quick peek around that next bend." We had been taking that "quick peek" for hours now.

The beauty and the silence of the place enveloped us. Ruin after ruin sheltered under the overhanging canyon walls, and Anasazi and Navajo rock art stared down at us on every turn. But in our eagerness we had endangered ourselves.

The footing in the canyon bottom grew even softer. The sand moved under our feet like ball bearings. We seemed to spend more time slipping backwards than going forward. Finally, Joe declared we had to find a way out of the canyon and get back to the car.

This hike was my idea. I had asked Benton Johnson, a Navajo artist who lived in the area near Many Farms, Arizona, if he had ever explored the pretty little canyon close to his home. I'd flown over it several weeks before with Chris Carson, a pilot from Chinle. From the air we saw a narrow, winding canyon that seemed to be boxed in on the eastern end. It snaked between rose- and maroon-colored cliffs for several miles, entered from both sides by numerous tributary canyons.

Chris flew low over the canyon, crossing it in a dozen places, then flew the main stream bed. We spotted several likely Anasazi sites, but now the canyon appeared to be totally devoid of humans and animals. I wanted to explore that canyon in the worst way.

Benton knew the canyon. "Oh, yes. That's what they call Skip Canyon. I've been in there. There's lots of ruins and a whole bunch of petroglyphs on the walls. My cousin's wife has the grazing permit for the canyon. I used to play in there when I was a kid. One of my cousins told me he was climbing around one day, way high up in the canyon, and came upon a soldier's body in a small cave. He crawled into this narrow place and just looked into a skeleton's face eyeball to eyeball." Benton laughed, "It scared him pretty bad. He was all by himself and he ran all the way out of the canyon. He said it looked like the soldier crawled in there to get away from someone and died."

This was my kind of a story. Imagine finding a soldier's body. This had the making of a real adventure. Benton talked casually about a dead body, which is not like a Navajo. Dead bodies are taboo. I asked him if his cousin knew whether the soldier were

American, Mexican, or Spanish. He didn't know. His cousin had crawled into lots of caves in the canyon looking for "things." Then he came face-to-face with a skeleton. He could see a uniform and a rifle but had been too frightened to investigate. Terrified is probably a better description.

My mind flashed back to accounts of the Spanish raid on Massacre Cave in Canyon del Muerto in 1805. Many innocent Navajos had been killed by an armed patrol commanded by Lieutenant Antonio Narbona. Spanish army units frequently prowled Navajo country during the eighteenth and early nineteenth centuries. Most had been punitive expeditions. Scattered Navajo bands, particularly in the Canyon de Chelly region, waged continual and ruthless war against Spanish, Mexican, and then American settlers. The Spanish and the Mexicans retaliated by raiding isolated Navajo camps deep in canyon country. Both sides gathered slaves, goods, and livestock.

Mexico gained its independence from Spain in 1821, almost three hundred years after Coronado's exploration. In that length of time, one might suppose the Spanish would have made peace with the Indians. No such luck. Isolated New Mexican ranches were fair game for armed and mounted Navajo war parties. On the other hand, Navajo camps suffered terribly from Spanish slaving raids. The Mexican government had little success in subduing the raiders, and when the United States acquired the territory in 1848, at the end of the Mexican War, it inherited the Navajo problem.

Navajo bands became stronger and bolder. Sheep and horses were a new measure of wealth, and clan chieftains ruled independently from each other. With civil war raging in the East, and even Albuquerque and Santa Fe briefly occupied by Confederate troops, the U. S. government called Kit Carson, the old Indian fighter, back to active duty. Ordered to solve the Navajo problem, Carson began a brutal campaign that eventually culminated in humiliating defeat and incarceration for most of the Navajo people.

We had a profound curiosity about the man who had died in the cave. Though we would not disturb his resting place, perhaps we might discover his nationality and which army or militia he served. I wondered why he was so far from Canyon de Chelly, the scene of many battles. Had he been a Navajo captive, or had he escaped from fierce enemy warriors only to die in a cave? If he had a rifle with him, I reasoned, he wouldn't have been a captive. But then again, I didn't know.

I told Benton that Dr. Wheat planned to come to Chinle for a visit to explore some remote areas. I assured him that we were not pot hunters, grave robbers, or pillagers. Of course, Joe would be very interested in seeing the small cliff dwellings in the canyon and photographing the petroglyphs.

I called Joe in Boulder and told him about Benton's story. He was excited about the soldier's story. The day after Joe's arrival in Chinle we decided to take a short hike into the canyon. Joe had suffered a heart attack the previous year and didn't want to overdo the exercise. But we forgot our concerns as soon as we got down into the canyon.

Benton had said there were many small cliff dwellings. We found one almost immediately, a three-room ruin in perfect condition. Adjacent to the ruin, petroglyphs covered the canyon wall. All had been chiseled into the soft, red rock, a sandy conglomerate easily carved with a sharp instrument. Close to the rock art, modern Navajo graffiti graced the wall with such undying declarations as "Susie Joe loves Willie Yazzie." It looked like a perfect party place for young Navajos, as well as a good place to keep livestock.

We finally came to an open, flat area near several larger ruins. It was a cool spot with large willow and cottonwood trees to shade us from the broiling sun. Joe spotted a faint trail that switchbacked up the slope to a rock overhang.

"I think if we can climb up to that overhang we can find a way over it to the mesa top beyond. What do you say, Jackson?"

It seemed possible. We had overplayed our hand and couldn't postpone our return any longer. I clawed my way up the slope, picking a trail for Joe. We paused frequently to rest and to scan the cliffs across the lonely canyon for sign of a cave that might hold the mysterious soldier's body. The air was still, and I was terribly thirsty. Joe's health became my foremost concern. Each time I stopped to rest I looked back. He seemed to be doing fine but I knew he had to be tired. I was worn out by the time we reached the overhang. Joe kept climbing steadily until we finally arrived at a ledge near the overhang. There we paused and talked about the soldier and enjoyed the view of the twisting canyon below.

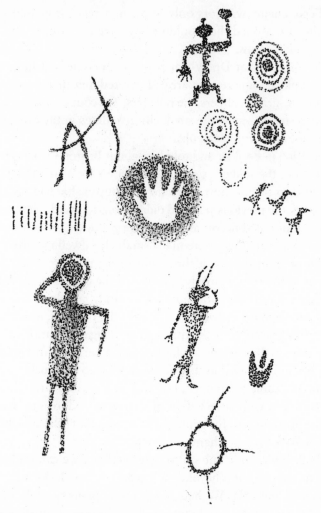

Rock art in Skip Canyon.

Fortunately, we found an easy route through a crack in the over-hanging rock and climbed out on top. We saw Joe's car far off in the distance. Joe suggested the path we had taken was probably an ancient trail in and out of the canyon. The canyon rim, or mesa top, was the same sandy red conglomerate we had found at the first ruin. It stretched for miles on either side of the canyon, broken only by the deep side canyons. Joe walked behind me and slightly off to one side.

Potsherds, Skip Canyon.

"Jackson! Look at this. Look at all these tracks cut into the rock. It looks like someone recorded a story by carving into the stone. It seems to be about a fight that happened here."

We knelt to look at the carvings cut into the rock surface. We could easily make out a jumble of footprints carved in an area only a few feet in diameter. The claw marks of a large bear merged with the tracks of one or two smaller bears. Two pairs of moccasin tracks, one the size of an adult and the other that of a child, were also carved in the rock. The moccasins walked to the spot where bears and humans seemed to mingle. Two people, maybe a father and son, had apparently come across a mother bear and two cubs. The hand-prints of a child and the adult were plainly visible in the group of bear tracks, but the child's footprints never left the scene.

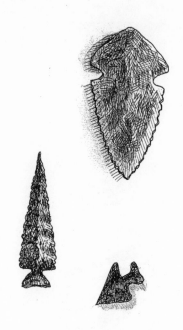

The tracks to and from the site were dim from years of erosion and eventually just faded out, obliterated by the wind and rain. A tragic story had been told in the rock, carved by someone who survived a struggle or who knew of the encounter. It was easy to imagine that the prints of bears and humans had been marked by blood and that the carving was done shortly after the struggle. Were the carvers Anasazi or Navajo? When did this happen? We had no answers. Joe said he'd never seen anything like it. Our time was limited, and we hurried back to the car vowing to return someday to attempt tracing the moccasin tracks to an ancient dwelling. None of the Navajo families living near the canyon had ever seen these strange markings.

Late that fall Joe and I went back to Skip Canyon on a cold, bitter day quite distant from the midsummer heat. We took along two young Navajo guides, Bennie and John, hoping to locate the soldier, photograph him, leave him undisturbed. Our guides knew where he was—or so they said.

I asked if they had any fear of going into the cave if we found it. John said he would show us the cave, but would not go in.

"My wife is expecting a baby. If I look at a dead person it will harm the child."

Bennie said he was a nontraditional Navajo and had no fear of the dead soldier's spirit. We walked up the canyon to the place

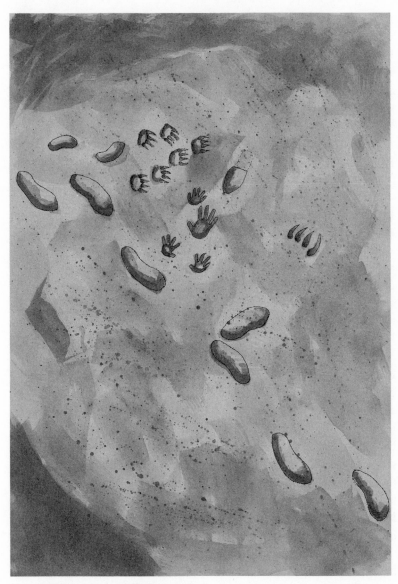

". . . only the adult walked away."

where Joe and I had climbed out on the first hike. Pointing to a steep cliff, Bennie said we'd have to use ancient toe holds to get up to the top, then walk along a narrow ledge to a side canyon. Another cliff-like slope must then be scaled. Joe and I tried it. After slipping and sliding on the "easy" part, we asked the two Navajos to go on alone. I don't like heights, and this was more than I wanted to tackle.

Both Bennie and John had been reared near the canyon, their playground. They scrambled up the steep slope and disappeared from sight around a bend. We watched, listened, and waited. Finally, after an hour, they appeared at the top of the lower cliff. Lightly as ballet dancers they skipped down the forty-five degree slope and approached us.

"Well, we got to the cave," Bennie said. "That's the place all right. I was there with the man who found the soldier first. But we didn't go in. It is just too dark, and I was afraid that there might be snakes in there. I'll get a flashlight and come back later when it isn't so cold. But that's the place. I'm not afraid of the soldier, but I don't like snakes."

We abandoned the search for our soldier for that day, choosing to walk up the canyon another mile where we found a dozen completely untouched ruins. All during the walk I thought about the soldier and the two Navajos. Was he really there? Were the two men sure that they had the right place, and would we ever uncover the riddle of the mysterious soldier? I felt keen disappointment. Secretly I hoped that we might find this uniformed warrior was a famous scout for Antonio Narbona of the infamous Massacre Cave incident. Perhaps in his pocket we might find important clues to Narbona's mission. I've always been a daydreamer, but this seemed more than a daydream.

I have been back several more times. Each time Bennie or John has an excuse. Perhaps we are not supposed to know about the soldier. His secret is secure. Maybe he has been disturbed enough.

Joe Ben Wheat and Navajo guides, Skip Canyon, October 1987.

Remembering Louis L'Amour

Like his books, Louis L'Amour was bigger than life, a man who wrote about big men and real places. He had fists like hams and biceps larger than many men's thighs: a well-proportioned fellow with the bearing of a man who knew what to do and how to do it when it came to the business of life. I knew him well.

We traveled around the Four Corners together, exploring new places and revisiting old ones. Many of his books and short stories had their setting in the remote mountain, desert, and canyon country on and off the Navajo Reservation. His book *The Haunted Mesa* brought Louis L'Amour and me together in the mid–1970s. It was a friendship that lasted until I moved away from Durango in 1987, only months before he died.

The L'Amour family spent a month each summer at the Strater Hotel in Durango, until they bought a condo at the Tamarron resort. A few years later they found Louis' dream ranch in a hidden valley not far from Durango. I had seen Louis and his family many times dining at the hotel but had never been introduced to them.

One morning, as I was leaving the Strater coffee shop, he hailed me. "I hear you know a lot about Indian art. I need to buy a painting. If you have a minute, take a seat and I'll tell you what I have in mind."

He outlined a story, the rough plot for a book about a man who builds a home on a remote mesa. The spot was once the site of an

Louis L'Amour in the La Plata Mountains.

ancient Anasazi dwelling. While the house is being built, the man begins to feel the presence of strange forces, a feeling that he is not alone on his mesa despite the remote location. One day his dog digs into a long-abandoned tunnel or passageway and disappears into an underworld.

"I'm looking for a painting for the jacket cover. Do you think you might have anything suitable?"

A painting by Navajo artist Clifford Brycelea came to mind.

"I think we have just the thing. Come over to our showroom in the Pepsi building when you have a chance," I replied.

That was the beginning of a close relationship with Louis. It was also a good break for Clifford Brycelea, as the painting Louis bought was used on the jacket. Clifford also illustrated several magazine articles for Louis during the intervening years. The two men became good friends. Louis was never too busy to share ideas with Clifford. In return, Clifford shared much of his knowledge of Navajo culture and mythology with Louis.

One time, while researching *The Haunted Mesa*, Louis and I hiked through a sagebrush- and cactus-covered wilderness, about twenty miles west of Monument Valley, looking for a mesa he had scaled decades ago. We parked my Saab on the side of the road and walked a hundred yards to a small hill.

"That's it. The long mesa just ahead. That's No-Man's Mesa. Look here on the map. Distances are deceiving in the desert. I'd say we must be two or three miles from it, but if we are where we think we are, the map says it's twenty miles away. That's one big chunk of rock." He scanned the mesa with his binoculars.

"I came from Navajo Mountain, down this arroyo directly to the base of the mesa. Here, you can pick it out on the map. I approached it on the far side. That's where I found the trail that took me to the top. Now, I'd like to find that trail again."

He explained that he had been trekking across northern Arizona on his way to a Colorado mining camp when he and several companions decided to climb No-Man's Mesa.

"It was just something that was there. We spotted a likely trail and crawled up to the top. I wonder if we can find it again. I'd like to get a little closer, but there's no time for it today. Let's drive down toward the San Juan River to see if a road winds around the mesa's west side."

We walked to the car, sinking ankle deep in the soft sand with every step, and drove toward the river on a seldom-used, rock-strewn, rutted dirt road, bouncing through dry arroyos and over rock ledges. It was like the rough roads I used to travel on back in the 1930s. But the Saab didn't have the stuff for the trip as those old Buicks did. We scraped bottom on the crest of hills and raked sagebrush along the car's smooth Swedish paint. Sand seeped in the tiny cracks around the doors. It was slow going every inch of the way. The mesa appeared to be no closer than when we had viewed it an hour earlier. Finally, a sandy wash stopped the Saab dead in its tracks, stuck solid.

After an anxious hour of pushing, shoving, and digging, we were able to back out. We were lucky: the last car we had seen was twenty-five miles back at Oljeto. We decided to head back to Durango and not chance any other mishaps.

"Jackson, that mesa has to have a route to the top. I have to find it. I have to find water up there, before I can write the book I have in mind. Let's charter a plane and fly over there tomorrow. Is that okay with you?"

"You bet your life it is. Jim Gregg will take us."

The following morning, Gregg, who owns a flying service in Durango, took us across the vast Navajo Reservation, over towering Shiprock, the Carrizo Mountains, Monument Valley, and abandoned World War II uranium mines, straight to No-Man's Mesa.

Louis pointed the way, and Jim's Cessna skimmed the mesa's rim high over the desert floor, tipping and banking so that I could photograph every portion of it. We made repeated passes, searching every imaginable place for a trail.

Louis pointed down to the mesa top. "See, Jackson, there's water down there. There are big water holes. It looks like they're fed by a spring from that cliff near where the canyon heads. But how in the world can you get there from the bottom? I climbed it, but I don't see how I ever did it."

We had spent the better part of an hour circling the mesa, flying as slow and as low as possible. We could see no sign of a trail to the top.

"Are you sure this is the same mesa, Louis?"

He shot me a glance. "Of course I'm sure."

One thing I learned was that Louis was rarely wrong about anything. He did his homework.

"Jim," Louis said to the pilot, "before we head back, let's go look on the north side of the San Juan River. There's a place over there called Johnny's Hole. I've noticed it on the map. I'd like to have a look at it."

Johnny's Hole turned out to be a maze of deep canyons and broad valleys, rimmed with sheer cliffs. Trails meandered through the peaceful setting. Huge cottonwoods grew in canyon bottoms. Fresh water flowed in a small creek that disappeared into the rocks. Paths through the sand indicated deer, mountain sheep, wild horses, and other animals knew the place. It was a green, beautiful spot, a Louis L'Amour place with no visible entrance or exit. The trees and other foliage contrasted sharply with the surrounding desert. We thought we could see ruins of several dwellings that might indicate Navajo or Paiute habitation, or maybe a settler's cabin.

Louis was fascinated. "I wonder who this Johnny was, or is. Look at the map. The place has a dotted line around it, like it is set apart from the rest of the country. That might mean it is private land. Do you know anyone who might know about Johnny?"

I have many friends in San Juan County, Utah, and if any of them knew, I felt sure I could talk to them. John Wetherill or Harry Goulding would surely have known, but they were both dead. I had a mission: to find out about Johnny's Hole. I never found a satisfactory answer. If Louis did, he never told me.

As we left Johnny's Hole, we skimmed a stark, barren mesa. It looked to be not over than a hundred feet in diameter, like a flat-topped volcanic cinder cone towering over Johnny's Hole. Louis pointed down at it. "Isn't that strange! It looks like it's burned to a crisp on top, like a rocket ship took off from there. Notice how it contrasts with the surrounding area. That's my mesa! That's my Haunted Mesa, the mesa in the book I plan to write. Look south across the San Juan—there's No-Man's Mesa. It's perfect!"

Louis liked people and always took time to make new friends. I went with him to many book signings. The only time I saw him angry was when a bookstore manager locked the door while people still waited in line. Louis admonished the startled fellow: "Those people are my fans! They bought my book and I want to talk to them." The book signing continued until the last fan had been greeted, the last book signed.

"Thank you, Mr. L'Amour" was always answered with "Thank you! You are my fans."

On my frequent visits to the L'Amour home in California, I saw the huge library file cabinets filled with documents and maps from all over the world. I marveled at the clutter on his vast desktop and wondered how he kept all the papers straight. Papers, books, clippings, and notes were everywhere. Brycelea paintings filled the walls and Navajo rugs covered the floor.

Many of Louis' fans incorrectly assume that he had a secretary, a research staff, and several assistants. He did the research and typing by himself. The finished work came off the typewriter without revision, page after page. One draft, and that was it. No rewrites. Kathy L'Amour, wife and best friend, proofread each manuscript before sending it to the publisher. If he got stuck on a plot, he'd put it aside for a time and work on another. I asked him about the books he had written while he worked on *The Haunted Mesa*.

"Well, Jackson, I got stuck on it for a while. I just haven't been able to get down in Johnny's Hole to satisfy myself about the setting, and I can't find a trail up No-Man's Mesa. In the meantime, I have deadlines to meet on stories I have had in mind for a long time."

Indeed, Louis had not been able to get down into Johnny's Hole. It beckoned yet remained forbidding and unreachable, as mysterious and remote as the first time we had seen it from the air. Between 1982 and 1987, in summer and winter, he tried to find a route to the mysterious place. He finally rented a helicopter.

No-Man's Mesa remained a mystery. In the summer of 1985 some of Louis' friends videotaped No-Man's Mesa from a slow-flying plane. Amazingly, the tape revealed three animals—horses or mules—grazing on the mesa top. No trail from the base showed up on the tape, but the animals knew the route. They couldn't live on the mesa during the bitter winter months, as there would be no food or water. I questioned all the traders and guides in the

Oljeto–Monument Valley–Navajo Mountain area. We never located the horses' owners or anyone who knew about them. The search for a solution to the mystery of No-Man's Mesa proved more frustrating than I had ever imagined. Louis speculated that a rock slide had buried the trail, perhaps leaving a tunnel. To this day I still do not know.

I marveled during these years that Louis would spend so much time on details.

"Why don't you just say that you know where the trail is and proceed with the book?"

"Jackson, I couldn't do that. My readers want to know that every place is real. To say that there was a trail, when none exists, would be dishonest."

When *The Haunted Mesa* was finally published, readers got to know the mesa as a strange and forbidding place. The hero never makes it to the top.

Louis and I talked many times about Navajo legends and witchcraft. I told him tales of witchcraft as I had heard them from people on the reservation. One night in the winter of 1983 Louis called me from Blanding. He had been on a midwinter mission to Johnny's Hole.

"Jackson, I want you to tell me again about skinwalkers, but first let me tell you what happened this evening, just a few minutes ago. I have just talked to a truck driver who came into the restaurant in Blanding where we were eating dinner. He had seen a strange creature out on White Mesa south of town. He came into the restaurant and asked what in the world was going on out there on that road. He described a creature that stood upright.

"It had the head of a wolf with blazing eyes and drooling mouth and the body of a man. He swears that the thing ran from the side of the road and raced right alongside his truck. Each time he slowed for a steep grade it tried to reach in the cab of his eighteen-wheeler. He couldn't pull away from it for several miles until he hit a downgrade.

"The fellow is terrified, almost hysterical. The sheriff, who was in the restaurant with me, says that reports of these creatures are not unusual. What do you think?"

A skinwalker on White Mesa! I knew lots about skinwalkers, but

I had never seen one. According to the Navajo, they are evil people, usually motivated by greed and jealousy, able to transform themselves into a werewolf-type creature. Sometimes called Navajo Wolves, they wear the skin of a coyote or wolf and prowl by night. The head of the animal serves to mask the wearer's identity.

I told Louis a few brief stories about Navajo weavers and silversmiths who had been witched or hounded by skinwalkers. These sorcerers are said to use corpse powder—ground flesh from a dead human body—to cast spells on whole families. To the Navajo they are real and nothing to be fooled with.

Nor are skinwalker encounters unique to the Navajo. I mentioned an instance in the winter of 1980 when one of our Pepsi drivers was returning from Mexican Hat on a back road over White Mesa. He was chased by a figure that appeared to be a wolf running upright as a human. This creature had tried to reach in the truck window. After that, none of my drivers would cross White Mesa at night.

Every book was an adventure for Louis. Writing was not work, it was his life. He looked forward to telling the stories he knew, and sharing them with his readers. He loved every moment at the typewriter, each story he could tell, each book he would write. He liked staying at the Tamarron condo, savoring the mountains and finding time to write. He was an early riser and would be at the typewriter from breakfast until noon. Occasionally he took a day off to go to the mountains or the desert.

I lived in Los Angeles for two summers in 1978 and 1979, and we planned lunch at least once each week. At the time I was driving a beat-up orange-and-white Dodge van, past its prime, scarred, battered, and bent. I'd pick him up at his home just off of Sunset Boulevard shortly before noon. We would talk briefly about a new book that had just arrived in the mail, look at a map, or inspect a spot on the wall where he wanted to hang a new Navajo rug or painting. Then we'd go to lunch. We'd arrive at the Beverly Hills Hotel's valet parking area in my old van and be treated as though I were driving a Mercedes. The parking valet took the van, and Louis and I would go to the Polo Lounge. His table was always ready.

Louis drank very little, but he loved good food. He made a real effort to control his weight, but to me he never seemed heavy. His height, well over six feet, and his big frame always seemed to accommodate his weight.

We never spoke of our own mortality, but it seemed to me that Louis was driven by a desire to write about everything he knew. One day we sat and looked out over a canyon in the La Plata Mountains near his Colorado ranch. He told me that he had so many stories to tell, but there was so little time. I don't think this was a premonition, just a realistic assessment. He was nearing his eightieth birthday. I asked about his research.

"I don't have a photographic memory, but I rarely forget anything I read or hear — unless I choose to. If I'm not sure of facts, I have a library, and I can look them up."

His memory was fantastic. He related names, dates, and geographic locations to me from his earliest wanderings. I heard yarns about a boxing match between him and a fellow lumber-camp worker. He told me of taking command of a Chinese junk when it was caught in a small typhoon off a southeast Asian coast and how the captain had failed in his duty.

"Someone had to do it. I didn't know much about sailing, but I knew it had to be done. I had to keep the ship off the rocks or we'd all die." Bigger than life, Louis took command.

In many ways, his own life was more remarkable than the lives of his heros. Yet, he seldom talked about himself, preferring to talk about the characters and plots for books. The one story he seemed to put off was his autobiography. There were more important things to do. He had too much to say, to write about, to be cast entirely as a Western writer. He worked for many years researching *The Walking Drum*, a tale set in thirteenth-century Europe and Asia, which became Louis' most popular work in Europe. Only in the last few months of his life did he begin work on the story of his life.

As I recall the many good times with Louis L'Amour, I remember most the gentleness of the man, his good nature, his wit and kindness. I saw him defeated only once in all the years I knew him. A power company planned to erect a high-tension power line across his ranch. Final approval was in the hands of the county commissioners. I had seen him address large gatherings, small groups of fans, and appear on national TV. At the commissioners' meeting, the cards were stacked against him, and he seemed to sense it. He entered the room, tall and erect, determined to present his case in a persuasive manner. Louis warned that this power line would emit radiation harmful to anyone who lived or worked nearby. He stated his case eloquently, presenting documentation to support his stand. He ended, "I'm a writer. My mind is my living. I can't afford to be 'zapped' by energy I know is harmful."

The hearing was a sham. That night in the dingy basement of a rural county courthouse I saw him nervous and unsure. I thought later that he was like a gunfighter from one of his novels who enters the saloon and knows he's outgunned. Louis had been at ease with President Carter, President Reagan, and the premier of France, but this was different. The good old boys wanted that power line across his ranch, and nothing would change it. Kathy L'Amour said that decision was the greatest disappointment of Louis' life.

Louis' thousand-acre ranch was the dream of his life, a great open place with room for elk and deer, and plenty of wild berries for bear. It was an isolated place with a soaring ridge to the south capped by Maggie's Rock, which he wrote about in *Passing Through*. I remember the many picnics in a grove of trees on the ranch. Louis dressed the part: boots, black hat, ever-present bolo tie, and a six-gun strapped to his hip. He never seemed to pause to eat at these gatherings. He was too busy talking to guests, sharing yarns, remembering old times, and planning new adventures.

He loved the old house, once a stagecoach stop, built from hand-hewn logs, nestled in a valley close to the highway yet hidden from view. Cherry Creek meanders westward through willows and cottonwoods; on the far side a lush meadow beckons. Of course there were bullet holes in one wall of the house, evidence of ancient gunplay. Here Louis wrote, walked, entertained, and thought—a treasured place lovingly restored the way he wanted it. Books filled the shelves; Navajo rugs graced the walls. The house had a lived-in feel about it.

He had planned to establish a library and research center on the ranch, a place where scholars and students from all over the world could work and use his library. Those dreams vanished when the power line was built. The library and research center were canceled. I think his heart was broken.

Just knowing Louis was an adventure. One bright autumn day

Louis L'Amour's favorite picnic area.

we sat on the crest of the pine-covered Lukachukai Mountains in the heart of Navajoland, not far from where my father had picked up the young Navajo from the CCC camp. We looked across a red-rock valley to a point just under an overhang. Louis spotted a cave in the rock, a big cave with a trail leading up from the valley floor. A roughly constructed rock fortification guarded the entrance to the cave. We speculated that it was a Navajo refuge, long abandoned and rarely visited. Louis' sharp eyes had located it; binoculars brought it closer.

"I'd like to take a look in that cave. I have a story in mind about a Navajo family who hid from the Spanish in such a place. Let's go there sometime."

We never got to go, and the story was never written. But to me, Louis L'Amour was always the bigger story, a real-life story of a big man with a big heart and a sharp mind.

Now he is gone, the typewriter is silent, and so many stories remain untold. Somewhere, beyond the far blue mountains, Louis is probably entertaining his companions with tales of his earlier life in a different place. I wonder if he got to take his big black hat, his boots, and his bolo tie.

"When I die, remember that what you knew of me is with you always. What is buried is only the shell of what was. Do not regret the shell, but remember the man." This quotation from *Last of the Breed* is surely what Louis said to all who were left behind.

Navajo Gold

Louise Tsosie, a skilled Navajo weaver, came to my house in Chinle with a pictorial rug rolled up in a flour sack. A shy young wife and mother, Louise seemed ill at ease. She had always met with me at Toh-Atin in Durango. Now she was in my home. I had only recently moved to Chinle. She asked more for her rug than I could pay.

It always takes time to buy a Navajo weaving. Sooner or later we'd find the right price. She knew it and I knew it. I poured her a soft drink while we visited about everything except the price of the rug. Every once in a while she'd glance at my Fisher metal detector propped in the hall.

Finally she asked, "Does that thing work?"

"Sure it works. Someday I'm going to find a lot of buried treasure and lost coins and, if I'm lucky, maybe a gold mine. Why?"

"Oh, I was just wondering. Jimmie's been thinking about getting one." Jimmie was Louise's husband. "How much do they cost?"

"They're expensive. Why would he want to buy one? Does he know about some treasure sites out here in the reservation?" I knew too many questions too fast would be uncomfortable for her to answer.

"Louise, maybe if he knew about someplace to go we could go together. Why don't you ask him?"

"Well," Louise replied, "You better talk to him. It's his business, and I don't know anything about it. I think that it has something to do with his grandfather."

We got back to the rug business and eventually negotiated a price. She was halfway out the door, money in hand, when she mentioned the detector again.

"You sure that thing works?"

"I guarantee that it works. I just don't know all that I need to know about it, but I'd sure like to talk to Jimmie. I have lots of time to go out treasure hunting if he'd like to go."

That was the end of the conversation. For the next few days I wondered about her interest. Finally curiosity got the better of me, and I headed off for the Tsosie house to try to talk to Jimmie about using the detector. I know that in such cases it is never wise to rush a deal. Navajo time is a reality, not just a catch phrase. I always tell people who are doing business with a Navajo artist to take it easy. It will all work out, or it won't. Big pressure has soured many a deal.

On the way to the Tsosie house I recalled all the stories about Navajo gold and silver; the lost mine legends, murdered miners, buried caches, and secret hiding places. I remembered tales of treasure found in old buildings, along dry arroyos, and under secluded cliffs. How about all those Spanish gold legends? Some of this had to be true, and Jimmie Tsosie might have some clues.

The Tsosie family lived in a modest home in a Navajo tribal housing development near Chinle. I parked by the back porch. Jimmie sat on the porch step tuning his drum for a peyote ceremony. He never looked up, never acknowledged that I'd driven up, concentrating instead on his drum. I remained seated in the car and waited. It is considered bad manners to knock on a door, honk the horn, or call attention to your presence in any manner until you have been greeted and welcomed.

Jimmie's drum, a curious looking contraption, was actually a cast-iron kettle with a piece of tanned cowhide drawn over the top. The kettle, partially filled with water, resonated eerily as he tilted it from side to side and tapped the hide with a small, padded stick. Deep muffled sounds changed to a high-pitched wail as he tilted the drum from side to side. The sounds were mesmerizing. I could only imagine the sensation if one were caught up in a peyote ceremony.

I might as well have been a thousand miles away as he continued testing the drum. Then, still not looking at me, he said, "Louise is not home. She went to Gallup with her mother."

"I wanted to ask her about the sandpainting rug she is weaving, and I wanted to talk to you too. Louise asked me about my metal detector. Did she mention it to you?"

"Yeah, she said something about it. She said you don't know much about it either. You ever find anything?"

He got me, I thought. Now I'll either have to lie or tell him I really don't know much about the thing.

"Well, I don't know too much about it, but I have found a few things, coins and a horseshoe out in the Apache country, a ring near my house, but I haven't found any treasure. I'd really like to look. Do you know anyplace where we can hunt? I have time to do it if you do."

Random treasure hunting on the Navajo Reservation can be risky. It is illegal on U.S. or tribal property unless an individual or family has knowledge of a personal trove. Digging for artifacts and pottery is off limits anywhere. But I didn't want any pottery. I wanted gold and silver!

Jimmie got up and walked toward the door. "Well, I might tell you something, but I am going to think it over. I'll come down to your house tomorrow."

Early the next morning, Jimmie, Louise, and their three sons turned up at the house. Jimmie didn't want to touch the detector at all. He wanted me to show him how it worked. We put some coins, a nail, and an aluminum pull-tab on the ground and got started. Even I was impressed.

I turned the discrimination control up, and we were able to find the coins in the tall grass. The discrimination setting allows the machine to reject the signal from unwanted metal items. It worked fine; the aluminum pull-tab and the nail were rejected. The machine gave off a loud tone as it passed over the coins.

"Will that find stuff that is buried?" Jimmie asked.

"Sure. How deep?"

Jimmie thought a minute. "Oh, maybe two, three feet. Way down there."

"We can try. It will either work or it won't. Tell me what we will be looking for."

He hesitated. "My grandfather, he's been dead a long time, was a rich Navajo cattle and sheepman. He used to buy and sell livestock. Lots of times he got paid in gold and silver coins. He took all the paper money and bought more livestock. He didn't have no bank so he put the coins in jars and cans and buried them out on his ranch."

"Where was the ranch, Jimmie?"

"Oh, he lived way out there by a bunch of canyons and hills. A long way from here." Navajos don't point, and Jimmie didn't specify which canyons, which hills, or which direction. He didn't want to give out too much information. It was okay with me. Navajo time. Jackson's time. I had lots of time on my hands—and lots of patience.

"Jimmie, if we are going to hunt for real buried treasure I'll have to get a better outfit. This won't do the trick for deeply buried items. It's okay for things close to the surface, but it's not reliable for items buried deep in the ground. Before I spend a bunch of money, I would like to know have you actually seen any of these coins?"

"Sure. One time, about ten years ago, my uncle was digging a posthole and he found a jar of gold and silver. It was out there on the ranch. I think there might be more. My grandfather's second wife told me that he had buried it all over the ranch. I just don't want anyone to know we're going out to look for it."

I think my heart actually skipped a beat. Hadn't he said, "We're going out there to look for it"? Of course he had.

That afternoon I called Carl Anderson, a dealer in Florida who sells high-tech treasure-hunting gear. I ordered a dowsing instrument, paying with a credit card. Several years ago a friend of mine had recovered a gold ring he had lost in a hay field. With a dowsing device, a small sample of the target substance such as silver or gold is loaded in a chamber on the instrument. I had heard that Anderson's Precision Master Rod might locate a target up to a city block away. An ordinary metal detector is good for pinpointing the exact location of metal objects, but it is useless over large areas. I had full faith in the Anderson technology. The cost was six hundred fifty dollars, a mere pittance when treasure is to be found. Navajo gold! Every treasure hunter's dream. Jimmie Tsosie and I would find it.

I had to know more about treasure hunting, so I set out to read every book, magazine article, and advertisement I could find. All bragged of finding buried gold and silver. I was so anxious I

Precision Master Rod: ". . . a sensitively balanced tool."

couldn't sleep. Though I had no experience with a dowsing instrument, and very little with a metal detector, I knew I could do it. When the Master Rod arrived, I practiced in my front yard and on various school playgrounds. I wanted to go up to Jimmie's house, rap on the door, get him out of bed so we could get going.

Jimmie and I agreed on a split in which my share would be twenty percent of whatever we found. Not much, but if lots of gold were involved, it would be plenty. If I didn't appear too greedy, we might have more chance of success. The main thing was to have fun.

I had no idea where we were going or how far we would have to drive over reservation roads. Joe Ben Wheat came to visit me in Chinle and volunteered to use his Jeep Wagoneer. When we got to the Tsosie home, Jimmie was waiting for us with his young son, Marvin. I had reservations about Marvin. He always seemed to get into my things when he came to the house, but if Jimmie wanted him to go along, it would be okay.

We drove eastward toward the large mountain range, down into canyons, over rock ledges, through sand dunes and sand washes.

We opened gates, closed gates, took the wrong trail a dozen times, and finally ended in the bottom of a canyon from which there appeared to be no escape. We couldn't move out of the canyon, even in low-range, four-wheel drive. I couldn't back up the hill on the trail we'd use, so Jimmie came up with a solution.

"This trail gets worse from here on. I think you'd better drive up the canyon, over those rocks, and then we can take another road up to the top. From there on it gets better."

We had no other choice. Up the sandy, rocky, debris-strewn arroyo we went, banging, scraping, and bouncing from side to side until we found Jimmie's trail. It was no superhighway, just a steep, narrow, rocky road. I'd been driving since we left the Tsosie home. I liked the Wagoneer. I pointed its nose uphill and gave it the gas, even if I couldn't see the trail over the long hood. I felt my way along, creeping up the grade, and finally made it to the top. From there we could see the deserted Navajo ranch.

"That's the place!" Jimmie exclaimed. "That's where we're going."

What a lonely, lovely place. A gentle, sloping plain stretched eastward toward the mountains and south to the rim of a deep canyon. Isolated? Yes. We were twenty miles from the highway. We might as well have been on the moon. The four of us were alone with only ghosts for company. Jimmie was emotionally involved in this ranch. His grandfather had controlled the place despite the almost universal custom of female ownership. The old man must have had a strong personality. We didn't talk much about it. He'd tell me later if necessary.

Jimmie said his grandfather didn't have a bank to put his money in. Even now, he wouldn't have one. The local bank in Chinle was closed down, with the nearest bank now in Window Rock eighty miles to the south. Something else his grandfather didn't have was neighbors. I could see one Navajo settlement way off in the distance, across a canyon and up a hill. It looked deserted too. I saw no livestock, no people, and no fresh car tracks. We were in the boondocks, in the middle of nowhere in Navajoland. Off to the east, the Carrizo Mountains broke the desert flatness.

Thunderheads began to build, ready to unload a heavy summer rain on the high mountains. I didn't want to get caught in one of those canyons, on one of Jimmie's favorite trails, when a flash flood hit. The air remained totally clear even as the storm clouds threatened. Not even the smoke from the continually burning "landfills" of Chinle or Window Rock marred the incredibly clear air. We saw the outlines of Monument Valley and the peaks of the Blue Mountains near Blanding. To the west, Black Mesa, sacred to both Hopi and Navajo, stood up from the desert floor. Grandfather's ranch was a beautiful place.

"How much land does your family control out here?" I asked.

"Oh, I don't know, they must have ten square miles or more. The family still has the grazing rights, and I'll start running cattle and sheep out here when I find the buried money." Jimmie was an optimist.

We eventually stopped in the middle of what had been a compound. One old house remained standing; the balance of the place was in shambles. The hogan was long gone. Only a ring of stones marked the outline. The corrals were down. An old hoist used to jack wagons and autos off the ground for repair had mostly rotted away. We located foundations for several other buildings.

"How long has it been since anyone lived here?" I asked.

Jimmie thought a moment. "My grandmother, who was really not my grandmother, she was the second wife, or maybe the fifth wife of my grandfather, died about twenty years ago. Nobody lived here since then. She died in the hogan, and I think they burned it down after that."

I was puzzled. "If she was old and just died a natural death they wouldn't have to burn the hogan, would they?"

"There was something funny about the way she died, like she wasn't sick or nothing. She just died. Then they have to burn the hogan."

Many times, if death is imminent, the sick person is moved outside the hogan. A death hogan cannot be used for human habitation. The ghosts of the dead will make it a place of fear and evil forever. Apparently there had been a mystery about the woman's death. Jimmie didn't want to talk about it.

"Okay, Jimmie, where do we start?"

"My uncle said that he was digging postholes over by that fence. I bet they buried it all along the fence line. There's a whole lot of money out there."

I noticed young Marvin's interest in my metal detector, my tape recorder, and my camera. Perhaps I should tell him to be careful? I forgot about it. I had treasure on my mind. Gold!

One of the cardinal operating rules for a Carl Anderson Precision Master Rod is to avoid the heat of the day, thunderstorms, and high winds. A sensitively balanced tool, it must be able to swing freely from side to side. Heat affects the delicate balance of sample chamber and target. Winds blow it off course. The wind stayed calm but I knew it would pick up later as thunderstorms rolled over the mountains. We could count on no more than an hour of favorable weather.

We picked out a pile of rocks that looked like a marker near the hogan foundation and watched the instrument swing slowly to the northeast. I walked in that direction. Jimmie marked a line. Suddenly the rod began to turn from side to side and then to swing in a circle. The instruction manual said that this would happen at a point over or near the target. Gold! Silver! The chamber was loaded with a bean-size piece of silver, but we hoped to find gold. My heart pounded. Jimmie ran for the shovel. Marvin piled out of the car and dropped my camera. Joe, the calm one, suggested that we move to the north to determine a point where two lines would intersect. That was a good idea, but Jimmie began digging where the rod had begun to circle with the determination of Long John Silver. Dirt flew and dust billowed. He uncovered a bit of charcoal and some rusty pieces of iron. Nothing else.

I plotted my other line and at a point barely three feet from the hole Jimmie had dug, we hit another target zone. Jimmie started digging and immediately found a mercury dime, then another, and finally a few pennies more than two feet down. Pay dirt!

But that was the end of it. We spent the remainder of the morning going over the area bit by bit. We dug holes and probed the desert floor with crowbars. We cursed and prayed and laughed, always trying to concentrate on the question: If you were an old Navajo where would you bury your gold? We all had different answers.

Young Marvin, who by then had thoroughly disassembled my tape recorder and unwound several hundred yards of tape, volunteered his opinion. "I wouldn't have buried it. I would have spent it in Gallup."

Soon the sun was high in the sky, the wind kicked up, and we called it quits. Subdued but undaunted, we vowed to try again. Everyone loaded things in the Wagoneer. We were ready to head for Chinle when Jimmie remarked, "Oh, one thing more. There was a Spanish army bunch that got ambushed by Navajos long, long time ago, over in that canyon. I know someone who found some old Spanish stuff over there. You want to see?"

Of course. If, indeed, there had been a Spanish, or even a Mexican army unit operating in the area, and there had been an ambush and massacre, Joe and I wanted to see the site. Jimmie said we would have to drive down through another deep canyon (another deep canyon?) to a level plain adjacent to still another deep canyon. From that point we would walk.

"My uncle found a sword, a bridle, and some uniform buttons down there."

"How long ago?" I asked.

"Oh, it been a couple years. Maybe ten. I don't know, but I know where it is."

What a wonderful time I was having. Despite the disappointment of not locating the buried gold, this was adventure.

"Let's go," I said. "Let's find it before the rain moves down from the mountain."

I noticed Marvin devoting his interest to my camera. What I didn't know was that Marvin had used up a full roll of film taking pictures of such significant items as an empty can, a rusty bucket, a fencepost, and a hole in the ground. I had no more film with me. Joe had wisely kept his camera safely tucked away in a locked case.

We moved quickly to get to the rim of the canyon and left the car. From there the bank down to the canyon floor was treacherous. Rock ledges had crumbled into tiny, marble-like bits that rolled under our boots as we scrambled down into the canyon, over a hundred feet deep at that point. Jimmie pointed out the waterhole at the bottom.

"That's the place where it happened, but they found the guns over there, where the canyon forks. The Navajos had a fort built there. I'll show you."

I asked Marvin to go to the car and get the Fisher metal detector. We wouldn't need the dowsing instrument.

Before Marvin returned Jimmie remarked, "These bugs are terrible. I'm getting eaten alive."

Bugs were chewing me up, too. Small, hungry, almost invisible gnats swarmed everywhere. They inflicted terrible bites. I later learned they are called "no see-ums." My legs were red and inflamed, the back of my neck on fire. We had to get out of there or be devoured by these critters. We worked our way up the sloping canyon wall to a point under the cliffs. The bugs were less threatening than they had been down nearer the water. We rested, applied some bug juice, and looked things over.

Jimmie motioned to the other side of the canyon, "See over there, that's a Navajo fort. See how rocks are piled up and windows left for shooting? It's a good place for an ambush."

We again scrambled to a point where we could cross the canyon to examine the fort. Walls of loose stones had been piled on top of each other with no mortar to bind them together. It was a perfect location to control entry to the canyon's west fork. Across the canyon, where we had been, another fortification stood almost hidden in a cave. It controlled the east fork. Any hostile group would be completely covered by the warriors in the two forts. Joe and I might be the first white men to stand at this very place and visualize the battle plan. After all, how many non-Navajos would have reason to be out here in this canyon? There were so many questions. How long ago was this raid? How many men were involved? What actually happened? Had the forts been used in hunting deer and antelope and really not built to ambush the Spanish? That seemed unlikely. Perhaps the forts were already built when the Spanish raiding party entered the canyon.

I tried to put myself in the boots of the Spanish commander to guess at his feelings as he entered the trap. I wondered where he and his men might have come from. Were they all Spanish or had there been Indian scouts? What was his objective, and did any of them survive? I could visualize pale young men, probably frightened out of their wits, riding into this canyon. This was the most remote territory of the Spanish empire. How lonely and forbidding it must have been two centuries ago.

Ignoring the bugs we moved into the canyon bottom again to work the area with the metal detector. I switched the machine on, put on the earphones, and pulled the activating trigger. The trigger was broken. It didn't work. Damn!

I shouted, "Marvin, what the hell did you do to the trigger?"

Marvin was long gone: out of the canyon and back in the car. We had no choice but to climb out of the canyon and give the whole thing up, at least for the day. I was fuming when the strenuous climb began, but by the time we had reached the car I had calmed down. The treasure hunt had its funny side, and we'd had a fine time. Jimmie was an entertaining guide, and we could always come back another day. I hoped the detector was not seriously damaged. The tape recorder might be repairable, and my camera was okay. Marvin crouched in the back seat when we reached the car, only his eyes moving. I did nothing. It was up to Jimmie. Jimmie was more interested in having lunch.

"Let's ride over to the top of that hill. That's where the soldiers camped."

A pretty fair road led to the top of the hill from the canyon, less than a mile from where we had crawled up from the forts. I got out the fried chicken, soda pop, and cookies. While we ate we looked over the area below us. Sure enough, this had to have been a bivouac site. It commanded the high ground, had a large, level area, but lacked fresh water. The water supply was in the canyon bottom, but from the high ground the forts were entirely hidden.

Jimmie said, "I know one of those guys who found all that stuff. I'll ask him to help me. I can't do it for a month or so because I have a job in Farmington, but we can come back sometime and find that gold."

We drove to Chinle. Everyone was tired, bug-bitten, and sunburned. The rain started to fall just after we hit the paved road. Giant thunderheads rolled over the Carrizos, the Chuskas, and Black Mesa. Lightning streaked across the sky. Jimmie, quiet for most of the drive to the Tsosie home, finally spoke.

"I'm glad we're not out there in that lightning." For Navajos death by lightning is death of the worse kind. "Maybe it was time for us to leave. Maybe something is telling us that this is not the right thing to do. Maybe we should just leave it alone for a while. But maybe we ought to come back and look again. Next time I'm not bringing Marvin."

Weavers, Witches, and Skinwalkers

A Navajo woman, whom I know only as Rose, interrupted my conversation with Larry, the trading post manager. She needed to talk to him that very moment. I'd seen her enter the small store and walk toward the office where Larry and I were talking. She pushed her way by me and spoke to Larry. Navajos usually aren't impolite or pushy. They don't butt in when two people are talking. Something was wrong, and I eavesdropped to see what it was.

"I need to have you loan me some money for that rug I been weavin'. I need it today. We're going to have a ceremony and it will cost over five hundred dollars."

Larry was as surprised as I.

"What's going on, Rose? What's happened?"

"I been witched by some people out where I live. They're skinwalkers and they just been comin' every night. Two nights ago my aunt died. There was nothin' wrong with her. She just died. We're all scared. I don't know what to do." Panic stricken by events beyond her control, she wanted to hire a medicine man for a ceremony. The conversation drifted from English to Navajo and back again. I went to look at some rugs in the rug room.

The woman left the store after about twenty minutes with some money toward the ceremony. Larry shared her story with me. He didn't know how to help her except with an advance of two hundred dollars. He suggested that she contact the Navajo Tribal Police to ask for their help.

Larry watched as the woman left the store. He shrugged and said, "I hear these stories all the time. It's probably just a bunch of neighbors trying to drive her off her place. There isn't anything I can do except to loan her some money and hope that she will bring the rug in when it is finished." He never mentioned it again, and I never asked.

I had been keeping a journal on witchcraft stories. Though the trader wasn't interested, I was. I wanted to talk to her, if she'd let me. Unfortunately, when I left the store Rose had already driven off.

I first heard about Navajo witchcraft when I was a teenager in the late 1930s. Most Anglos didn't take it seriously. Bruce Barnard, a respected trader in Shiprock, first told my family about Navajo witchcraft. We had stopped by to see him in Shiprock on the way to the reservation. Dad wanted to know if he knew of any dances or ceremonies we might see. Barnard said we might run into a Yeibichai dance out near Red Mesa. Then in an almost off-handed way he said he had talked to a family who claimed they'd been witched. They had seen strange creatures like werewolves around their hogans. The family had pawned some jewelry with Barnard to get money for a sing to rid their place of evil beings.

"They live out there near Sweetwater. But I don't think you'll be able to attend a ceremony like that. I don't think there is much truth to it. I think it's all motivated by jealousy and greed. These stories have been going around for years. But I'm curious and I'd like to know a lot more about it."

The witchcraft story seemed farfetched. We didn't talk about it again, but I kept the story in the back of my mind and even wrote a paper on it for a junior high English class.

In the late 1950s, after I had started trading in earnest, I heard more and more about witchcraft. At Toh-Atin we had a bulletin board in the office to display Navajo weavers' photos along with each new rug they sold us. We thought of it as a hall of fame, but the weavers were horrified. Several weavers asked me to take their pictures down "because some witch will see it and do somethin' bad to me." One weaver said, "My sister came here last week and saw my picture on your wall. She said a neighbor of ours was staring at it. We think she is a witch. That same night I got real sick and couldn't figure it out. You gotta loan me some money and you gotta take all those photos down."

"How'd she know the person was a witch?" I asked.

"She just knew. You don't have to be told. You can look at a person and tell."

The hall of fame came down that same day.

I wanted to learn all that I could about witchcraft, so I bought a copy of Clyde Kluckhohn's *Navajo Witchcraft*, written in the 1940s and now something of a classic. Kluckhohn did research on the reservation beginning in 1922 while he was still a college student. Fluent in Navajo, he used to pick up hitchhikers on reservation roads. After he'd gained their confidence, he'd ask them what they knew about witchcraft. I decided to copy his method. A soft drink, a snack, and a pack of cigarettes would loosen tongues. I talked first about the weather and their families, and persuaded them to teach me a little of the Navajo language. Soon we'd be laughing and telling stories. My pronunciation often provoked giggles and laughter. Then, and only then, did I bring up witchcraft. I would start out by saying something like, "I was talking to a lady from Tuba City (or some distant place), and she said that she had a lot of witches over there. Do you have any witches up where you live?"

The first time I tried this, my passenger, a man in his early 40s, asked to be let out of the car. I stopped, and he got out without a word and put his thumb up to attract another ride.

Interrogating strangers was okay, but it was much more interesting if I knew the person I was talking to. I began questioning Navajo weavers, silversmiths, and their families who came to our showroom. I knew them, and they knew me. Many seemed glad to talk and didn't hesitate to tell about their experiences with skinwalkers and witches. Talking about it seemed to be a form of therapy. I asked traders, anthropologists, and doctors, all of whom had years of experience on the reservation, about witchcraft. Slowly and surely the pattern began to develop. Yes, witchcraft is a fact of life for many Navajos. But as far as I was concerned an isolated story didn't make a pattern. However, as I continued my interviews, the pieces began to come together.

Many reservation dwellers, Navajo and Anglo alike, don't care to discuss witchcraft at all. One Navajo friend of mine refused to talk about it at all. We had worked together several times at Indian art shows in various museums and galleries. Sometimes I was asked to give a talk on witchcraft. When he heard about it he'd simply leave the building. He bluntly asked me not to question him about it anymore, saying it was too close to discuss it. Then, months later, he came to my office unexpectedly.

"I think I better tell you about this witchcraft thing. Then you won't be questioning me anymore. This is hard for me to talk about, but my grandmother was a witch. Some Navajos found out about it and they came after her in broad daylight. They chased her on horseback until her horse dropped from exhaustion. When they caught her they killed her by driving a stake through her heart. Now you understand why I didn't want to talk about witches."

Obviously, not all Navajos believe in witches and witchcraft. However, it is safe to say that even the most "enlightened" Navajo is aware of specific strange happenings related to witchcraft. It has nothing to do with Navajo religious beliefs.

In studying the Navajo, indeed, the entire Southwest, it is necessary to remember how isolated the colonies of New Spain, now Arizona and New Mexico, were from other cultures. Santa Fe was the most remote outpost in all of New Spain. The Spanish, for the most part, were not benevolent conquerors. Most were adventurers from Spain and Mexico, more interested in treasure than the health and welfare of the native population. The Spanish colonized, Christianized, and exacted tribute for the Spanish Crown. They brought their own tales of witches and witchcraft along with their superstitions, the Catholic church, and the Inquisition. It is amazing that native faiths of any sort survived the turmoil of the conquest and subsequent colonization, especially since native ceremonies were banned. In fact, most native languages and religious customs survived centuries of Spanish, Mexican, and American domination and are intact today.

From my personal experience strange things do indeed happen on the reservation—things that I can't understand.

I know white men who have seen skinwalkers at night near Chinle and Kayenta and, in the case of Louis L'Amour's truck driver, near Blanding. I know Navajo women who have had strange

animal-like creatures run alongside their cars on dark nights on lonely roads. A Navajo nurse told me that a skinwalker jumped up on the rear bumper of her Volkswagen as it bumped along the dirt road between Chinle and Nazlini.

A young Navajo artist told of his fear of witches. He said, "I never believed in these things until I became a success in my work. Now we have people asking all of the time how I can have a new truck and why I don't have to go to work every day.

"I'm not sure that I believe in this witchcraft thing even now, but I am taking no chances. I don't want my family to be hurt by some jealous person—witch or not. I'm putting some pieces of wood that a medicine man blessed over every door and window in my house. And we are leaving the outside lights on all night.

"My cousin saw a skinwalker at the school he works at. He had just driven into the school yard when he saw it over by the fence. My cousin was afraid but he decided to try to run over the thing. He put the truck into gear and tried to catch it. Then, all of a sudden, the skinwalker jumped right up in the air and over an eight-foot fence and ran off into the darkness."

I believe that something is real. Something is happening, even in this enlightened time.

Bessie Morgan and the Skinwalkers

Bessie Morgan had been witched. Her letter told me about it: "Everything is fine down here except I need to see a medicine man and to have a ceremony. I've been witched. We been having a bunch of skinwalkers coming around here and they made me sick. Can I borrow $2,000?" Just as simple as saying, "I have a cold and need to see a doctor."

Like most Navajo families, the Morgans had no telephone. I couldn't rely on a message through a third party, so I decided to drive to Wood Springs, on the Navajo Reservation two hundred miles from Durango. I had no way of knowing if anyone would be at home when I got there, but I arranged to borrow the money and leave early the following morning. To get two thousand dollars in such a short time required hasty negotiations.

I was straightforward with my friend Nick Turner, the banker. "I got a letter from one of our best weavers. She's been witched. I need a loan so she can hire a medicine man for a ceremony to heal her. She needs to continue to weave. We have a lot of money invested in her rug, and it's less than half-finished. Why don't you take the day off and ride down with me?"

He frowned, rubbed his chin, and stared at me in silence. Perhaps he thought I was playing some kind of practical joke on him and he was waiting for the punch line. After what seemed hours, he laughed and said, "Thanks anyway, but I'll pass on the trip. Jackson, this isn't exactly a car loan, but we can work it out. I always know where I can find you. You do get into some of the damndest deals. If you don't pay it back we'll just hire a witch."

I drove rapidly the entire distance. I didn't want Bessie's family to leave for Gallup or Window Rock before I arrived. Fortunately, Bessie and two of her daughters were in the weaving hogan when I drove up.

"Hi there," I greeted them. "I got your letter and want to talk to you about the money."

There was a flash of disappointment on the girls' faces. Then Margaret, the younger daughter, said, "Well, you come on in and look at this rug. My Mom's been workin' every day on it so you can have it for your business. If you want to talk about it we can talk, but we really need the money. Awful things been goin' on 'round here."

I got my usual carton of Pepsi out of the cooler in the car. We popped the lids on the frosty cans and sat on the floor in front of Bessie's loom sipping the cold drinks. I had a chance to look at the large rug. It was superb, much better than I had expected. It had already been eighteen months since she started weaving it. I looked around the humble room and marveled that a fine artist could create such a lovely piece of art in such a place. For the first time I noticed that the floor was dirt, covered with a cheap carpet that bulged and dipped on the uneven surface. The ceiling was unfinished. The rough wood rafters looked to have been salvaged from an older building. It was a shabby room, but spacious enough for the large loom.

I thanked them for writing and then said, "You know I have been interested in this witchcraft thing for a long time. You always told me that you didn't know much about it, and now, all of a sudden, it's a big problem. What happened?"

Margaret answered, "Well, everyone knows about this big rug, and they think they know how much you gonna pay for it. They're just jealous, that's all, just jealous. They don't want my Momma to have that much money, so the skinwalkers come every midnight to scare us.

"It all started last month when we saw a big fire over there in those trees, not too far from the road. Then we heard all this whoopin' and hollerin' and funny words in Navajo. We all got afraid and turned off the lantern [they had only gasoline lanterns at that time] and sat on the floor. That didn't help much 'cause we saw the light from the fire and heard the noises all the more.

"Then we heard something on the roof. The whole place was shakin' and they were messin' around with the chimney on the stove. We heard them drop something down the stove pipe and we really got scared 'cause some people tell us that they put parts of dead people down the chimney, and that puts the whole house under their spell. I just shiver when I talk about it."

Bessie and the other girls nodded in agreement.

"Then, alla sudden, there was a noise by the door. Someone was trying to turn the knob, but I'd locked it. They just pounded on the door and then on the window. I saw this head by the window. It was the head of a wolf or coyote, and I really got scared. We saw his ears stickin' up and saw his breath too, 'cause it was a cold night. His eyes glowed red like an animal. The only light was from the fires those guys set, like I told you, but I could see that it was a skinwalker. I had never seen one before, but I knew what it was. There was a bunch of them. They just kept scratchin' at the window, but like they really didn't want to come in. They just wanted us to be scared."

"Why?" I asked.

"Like I said, jealousy. One of them kept saying over and over again, 'Bessie, don't you weave no more. You're takin' money from the people. Bessie, don't you weave no more. You're taking money from the people.' Over and over again."

"It's like some kind of primitive Marxism," I muttered.

"I don't know nuthin' about that. They just don't want Momma to weave no more. They think she's takin' money from the people by gettin' paid for her rug."

"That's what I said, Margaret. They think that the money Bessie is going to earn should be split between all the people. What time did they come? How many times have they come?"

"Oh, dey come 'bout once a week, always about midnight, but never the same day of the week. They start the fires and get to whoopin' and hollerin', and we turn off the light."

"Why don't you get a gun and shoot them?'

The girls looked at Bessie, and Bessie looked at the girls. Margaret answered in an incredulous tone, "Oh! We couldn't do that. They might be friends of ours."

"Then tell me why she needs the money. What can a medicine man do?"

"Well, she got shot with a piece of turquoise last week when these skinwalkers were not here. She was weavin' and then she heard this noise outside the window and a blowin' sound like someone was blowin' something out of his mouth. She got this sharp pain under her left arm and can't use it to weave or lift anything. One of those Navajos who tells you what's wrong, we call them handtremblers, told her that she had been shot with a piece of turquoise and that a medicine man is gonna have to suck it out. We are gonna have a ceremony and he will do a sandpainting and get that turquoise out of there."

"And this is going to cost that much money?" I asked.

Helen replied, "That's right. Without the ceremony she might die, and she can't weave 'cause her arm is no good. If she's sick who's gonna finish the rug? You gonna loan her the money?"

"Sure. We want her to feel better and finish the rug."

"Okay, then, we'll get the medicine man and have a ceremony."

Bessie was taking this all in, but saying little. It was apparent that she understood everything being said but knew it was better for her daughter to communicate with me. I left shortly after this brief conversation and drove back to Durango. The whole event seemed unreal to me. I wondered if my intense interest in witchcraft had triggered the Morgans' request. I didn't know, but time would tell.

Several weeks later I returned to the modest Navajo dwelling. Bessie looked wonderful. Her fingers flew over the warp of the large rug. It was like she was playing a harp and making it sing in silent harmony. Everything was in balance. The girls looked better, the home was neater and better kept, and there was a pride in Bessie's weaving that had been missing last time.

Helen whispered to me, "Now we know some of those people and who they are. The crystal gazer who came with the medicine man had us look in a crystal. We saw these two women moving around the hogan, like they were in a cloud. I never did anything like that before, but it was just like TV. Real scary. We could see them and know what they were doing. They were going to bury something near the door, but they didn't do it. It looked like they were scared. It was sorta like a video, only not too clear, but clear enough to know who they are. Then the next day they came to see my mother and see how she was feeling.

"They wanted to see the big rug, and I told Momma not to let them go in the weaving room without her, but she says it's okay. I got real nervous. I knew they would do something to the rug. Momma said that we had to find out for sure if they were the people who were jealous of her. Right after they left we went in the weaving room and found four warps had been cut. It was awful. The warp snapped down into the rug and it took Momma two days to get it through the weft threads and tied up again. I cried. She had worked so hard on that rug. Momma said, 'Now we know for sure.' Then the next day there was a finger from a dead baby on the door step of the weaving room. That's scary for us. Why do they do that?"

"Who are they, Margaret?"

"They are neighbors, and one is my mother's cousin. You know her. She sells rugs to you."

I was shocked. "Does she come over to your house anymore?"

Bessie turned from the loom and said, "Only at midnight, only at midnight."

Connie Bitsue's Ordeal

Connie Bitsue looked like approaching death. Her smooth, dark skin was drained of color. The purple circles hanging under her eyes made her look twenty years beyond her thirty-some years. There were heavy lines on her face and she had lost weight. The Connie I knew was a pretty, vivacious Navajo wife and mother bubbling with enthusiasm and charm. This day she looked as if she had seen a ghost—or was about to become one.

Shocked, I asked. "What's the matter with you? You look like you've been ill. What's happened?"

Connie's hand trembled. In her soft Navajo voice she replied, "Oh, we been havin' terrible things happen. We've all been sick, real sick. The house is cold and damp all the time, even when we have a big fire in the stove. Then, last week I wrecked my new car, the pretty red one you saw last month. It just ran right off the road like I didn't have control over it at all.

"Then, William's been actin' real funny, and last Monday, all of a sudden, he left home and went to Gallup. He's been in a bar for days. I'm real worried. I went to see one of those Navajo guys who tell you if you have a sickness or something. I think they're called handtremblers. He told me that we had all been witched. He said we have to have a ceremony to get rid of this stuff. I need money to pay a medicine man. I hope you will buy lots of jewelry and maybe loan me some money. We just gotta get rid of this witchin'."

When Connie mentioned "witchin'," my ears perked up. I had seen Connie at least once a month for several years. Until that day I never gave a thought to the fact that she might believe in witchcraft. She always concentrated on doing business and taking care of her family. There seemed to be no room for the supernatural in that family. Connie traveled on the road selling her husband's jewelry. William, the husband, was an innovative and talented Navajo silversmith who created exquisite pieces in gold, silver, and turquoise. I knew them well. They supplied fine jewelry for our business, and we had become friends as well. We had worked together at Indian shows, fund-raising events for museums, and art gallery events all over the country.

Elena, Connie's vivacious younger sister, came into the gallery and stood close to Connie. I asked her what was going on at the Bitsue home. Elena smiled and shrugged, saying, "Oh, I don't think that it's anything. That witching stuff is old-fashioned and superstitious. I can't believe in it, but I really don't know why the house is so cold and wet feeling all the time, and why Connie's car ran off the road. I was following her in my car and she just went off the road. There was no reason for it to happen. She got a bad bump on her head when the car rollled over. William hadn't been drinking much until the wreck. Now he's just hanging out at a bar in Gallup. Maybe he's just been working too hard, but he hasn't been home in three days."

I had a customer who had been waiting for one of William's gold belt buckles. Connie had it with her. I left the room to call my customer. I could hardly concentrate on my pending sale. Connie's story bothered me. I was sincerely concerned about her. When I returned to the trading room I asked her if her family had ever had trouble with witchcraft in the past.

"No, we never been bothered before, but some of the older people in the family tell us that things like this used to go on all the time. I just thought they might be old-fashioned."

We bought a large order of silver and gold jewelry from Connie and advanced her several hundred dollars in cash against future purchases. Connie and Elena left our showroom, got into their pickup, and drove away. Connie sat in the passenger seat, hunched over like an old lady.

Sande Bobb, our buyer, and I discussed Connie and the change that had come over her. Connie kept coming to mind over the next few weeks. It seemed to me that a dear friend was falling apart before our eyes.

One day, a month or so later, Connie and Elena came into the showroom again. This time Connie was bright, pretty, and full of pep. Elena, on the other hand, looked pale and frightened. The dark circles that had rimmed Connie's eyes seemed to have moved to Elena.

I asked Connie, "What happened when you went back home?"

Elena, who was as tense as a bowstring, spoke first, "I don't know what happened, but I want you to buy lots of jewelry. Buy as much as you can so that Connie and William can pay me what they owe me. I'm going back to college in Flagstaff, and I'm never going back to their house again. I'm going to graduate and move to L.A. It's too scary out there where they live."

I looked at Connie hoping that she would talk about it. She just kept taking jewelry from her sample case and talked about everything except what had happened since she left the last time. Finally, I asked her to tell me about it.

"Well, we got a medicine man and we had a ceremony in the hogan next to the house. We got the whole family in there, kids and all, and William's uncle, too. The medicine man got the place real hot from the fire in the stove in the middle of the room. We all sat around in a circle while he did all his singing and chanting. He brewed up some special tea that smelled like sagebrush. I'd never been to a ceremony like this. After a while he drew a little sand-painting on the floor, just like they used to do with colored sand and stuff. It wasn't a great big sandpainting like they use in some of the ceremonies, just a little one with some *yei* figures in it. Then he passed the tea around and we all took a drink from the bowl. It was real bitter tasting.

"The medicine man kept singing and chanting. It was like he was in a dream, or something. He just weaved back and forth. His voice was hypnotizing us. Then, all of a sudden, he took this rock, I guess you'd call it a crystal, from his case and held it up to his face and looked in it. The crystal was about the size of a football. He looked for a long time, then passed it on to William who was seated on the floor to his left. William turned pale and his hand began shaking and he passed it to me.

"I looked at the crystal which was all lit up and bright. I saw things moving around. I saw a man kneeling down by my car and then digging a hole in the road near our fence. It was just like I was watching TV! Just like TV! He dug a hole and put a deer antler in the ground under my car. Then he buried a bone that looked like a human leg bone, in the road. It was wrapped in something like hair or rope.

"I said to William, 'I know that man! I know him!' He is a Navajo who does silver work but isn't very good. He is always bugging us for money and wants William to teach him to make good jewelry. We don't like him so we never've been friends. But there he was, putting that antler under my car and burying that bone. I saw it in that crystal. Just like it was TV!"

I looked at Elena, who had been listening. She was crying.

"I know that it was all too scary. I want to get my money, and I'm going to leave and go back to college and never go back there again."

"Did you look in the crystal, too?"

Tears ran in rivulets down her cheeks.

I asked, "What the hell is happening here? I can't believe that everyone, all of you, saw these things in that rock."

Elena said, "We all looked in it. It was just like TV. I'm still scared. William said after we got through with the ceremony that he would talk to the man we had seen in the crystal. When William talked to him he didn't say anything except to tell William he had not done us any harm. He said he didn't know what we were talking about.

"William went to the garage where they had towed my car and found the steering rod had broken. It just broke. For no reason at all, it broke. It was a brand-new car. That's what caused my wreck. William dug up the bone that we saw in the crystal. It was all wrapped in human hair with a piece of turquoise tied to it. That's what made William get sick and go to the bar and drink. We never did nothing to that man. Why would he hurt us?"

Elena stopped crying. "I think he's just jealous. Connie and William have a new car, and William sells lots of jewelry. The kids have good clothes and toys. This guy wants to get even for some reason. It's really scary, and I don't like it. Come on, Connie, let's get back home before dark. I want to leave for Flag tonight."

Several months passed. Elena went back to college. William continued to craft fine jewelry. Connie sold more and more of it on the road. We also continued to buy it. But Connie was reluctant to talk about the ceremony or the man who seemed to have it in for them.

Then I met the man who had witched the Bitsue family. It happened at the Gallup Intertribal Ceremonial where Toh-Atin had a sales booth, along with fifty or sixty other dealers in Indian art. Our display of Navajo rugs, kachina dolls, and jewelry was off the main traffic aisle and against the back of the new exhibit hall.

Late on the final day, Sunday, I noticed a tall Navajo man and a sharp-faced Navajo woman concentrating on William's jewelry. Most of their attention was directed at a gold and turquoise brace- let. Jean Tipotsch, the head salesperson for Toh-Atin, asked if she could help them. She got only a dark and ominous look from the woman. The man never looked away from the bracelet.

Jean whispered in my ear, "Watch that Indian couple over there. They give me the creeps. The woman just keeps staring at William's bracelet and belt buckle. I think that they are up to something. It gives me the creeps. I'm going to get out of here for a while. You talk to them. Okay?"

I smiled at the couple. They glared at me. I asked if I might help, and the woman pointed to the bracelet. I removed it from the showcase and handed it her. Her hair, black as coal, hung down to the middle of her back. Her skin, lighter than most Navajos, accen- tuated her jet-black eyes, which had a brooding, sinister look to them. She didn't look at the bracelet but closed her eyes and grabbed it and held it tightly in cupped hands with only the tur- quoise and a bit of silver exposed. Her knuckles turned ivory as the blood drained from the pressure of her grip, squeezing the life out of the work. I glanced at the man who stood next to her. He had his hand clamped on her shoulder, eyes open, fixed on the jewelry. Fi- nally, pale as a ghost, she opened her eyes, and looked at me.

I had to say something. "Nice bracelet, huh? The silversmith is William Bitsue."

She handed the bracelet to me and snapped, "I know who made it. You didn't have to say anything." She glared again and turned away. I watched them disappear into the crowd. They had been at our booth for only a few minutes, but it seemed like hours.

When Jean returned to the booth, we discussed the pair and their behavior. She thought they might be the witches, the people who had brought so much pain to the Bitsues. I knew I had encountered two evil people. I'd have a chance to talk to William and Connie when they came to Durango next time.

Weeks later they brought some jewely up to Toh-Atin. I told them about the strange pair.

William shrugged and asked, "When did you say this happened?"

"Saturday afternoon, at the Ceremonial."

William reflected briefly, then said, "I knew something was happening about that time. I got a bad headache and felt weak all over. I thought that it was because I was working too hard. But it didn't seem like that. It seemed more like someone was telling me not to make jewelry anymore. I felt bad all day and all night. Now I know my neighbor caused it. They will never stop trying, but we have lots of power now from the ceremony and the medicine man. We are going to be alert because they might do something to the kids. Isn't she a wicked looking woman?"

Connie looked pale and tired. She asked William to get a box from the truck and bring it in. He left for a few moments and returned with a small box.

"This thing in here is a broken Anasazi pot I found in our tool shed," Connie said. "This belonged to a dead person. It is bad medicine for it to be near our house. I know those people you saw in Gallup put it there, and I don't want it. We wrapped it in a deer skin and put some corn pollen in the box so we could bring it up here. Things like this don't bother you, but they are bad for us."

The pot, a rather common and unremarkable example, had been broken into several pieces. I asked where it had come from.

William said, "I think those people dug it from a ruin near our house. We knew there was Anasazi stuff up there, but it's bad for a Navajo to get too close to a ruin. Things like that will make you sick. We just didn't want it around. Maybe you can use it or give it to someone."

The pot is still in the box. It's on a shelf in a storage shed, far from Navajo eyes, and out of my sight as well. I think I'll leave it there.

Ghostway

Mary Begay's youngest daughter, Lucy, hailed me at a gas station in Window Rock on a cold November afternoon in 1987.

"I'm glad I ran into you," she said. "We're having a ceremony for my mom this week. It started last night, Friday, and will probably go on for five nights. She's been feelin' real bad. We found a medicine man who says he can help her. We told your son we'd let him know about it because he loaned us the money. We didn't reach him, so why don't you come? It goes on all night, but you don't have to stay if you get tired."

I replied, "Thanks very much. I can't come tonight, so which night is best?"

"Oh, I think Tuesday night is the time to come. It's the last night, and lots of things will be going on that night."

Later that same afternoon I drove to the Begay home to get more details. Betty, one of Mary's five daughters, was working in the yard. She greeted me warmly.

"We been going to call you about the ceremony for Mom. We just didn't do it, because we don't have a phone, and I always forget it when I'm in town."

"That's okay. Lucy told me about it when I saw her in Window Rock. I'll be here Tuesday, if you're sure it's okay for me to come."

"Sure. It's fine. We're going to start sometime after dark. Maybe five or six o'clock. Sometimes they start later, but the medicine man says that he wants to get this going earlier. He's really tired. This ceremony is a lot of work. He's got to know all those songs and chants by heart, and he's got to feel good so he can put all his power into the ceremony. It's sort of boring, but it's spooky too. He and my mom are resting in the big hogan, over there."

She nodded toward the large hogan, an imposing building, situated on a low hill overlooking the houses in the family's compound. It had been finished in 1985 and rose over the dilapidated older house that had been the family home for years. Next to the old house was a new double-wide mobile home. Large piñon and juniper trees sheltered the three structures. Six churro sheep rested in the pen a scant fifty feet from the trailer. The whole family lived in this group of buildings, including the hogan, used only when all the daughters were home from college. The compound was off the paved road on an unimproved side road, which, predictably, was nearly impassable in wet weather.

"What can I bring?" I asked. "Food? Soda pop? Just tell me."

"We've got everything we need. Your son and daughter loaned us the money. That's enough."

I was delighted to be invited to a ceremony, but somewhat apprehensive. I didn't know what to expect, or, for that matter, what would be expected of me. I didn't even know which ceremony had been planned.

I left Chinle on Tuesday about five o'clock in the afternoon and drove straight to the Begay place. It was almost dark when I arrived. A cold wind blew from the north. It whipped the trees and sent leaves and trash scurrying around the yard. Lucy, busy chopping firewood in the yard directly in front of the hogan, greeted me when I drove up. "I'm just gettin' some wood for the fire. Mom and the medicine man are in the hogan, but you can go in and talk to her if you want to. She's pretty tired. This ceremony's been going on for days now."

I entered the hogan, taking a few minutes to let my eyes adjust to the dim light. One low-watt bulb hung from a cord near the door. Mary recognized me.

"Hello, we been waitin' for you. Where's your son?"

"I'm here by myself. He didn't get the word in time. I'll be the only one from Toh-Atin. Is there anything that I can do while we're waiting?"

"Well, we need some of that diet pop. I'm not supposed to drink things with sugar. If they have some pies at the store in Ganado we would like a pie or two, and maybe some chips and cookies, too."

The medicine man lay curled up on a thin mattress next to Mary. His eyes were open but unseeing, as if he was deep in meditation. He didn't acknowledge my presence in any manner.

I left the hogan, walked to the trailer house, and knocked at the door.

"Hi. It's just me, Jackson. I'm going to the store in Chinle to pick up some pop and a few other things Mary wants. What else do you need?"

One of the girls called out from the kitchen, "Bring some of those pies and some regular pop. We don't like that diet stuff."

"Mary told me she can't have sugar."

"Well, I want something with sugar in it. You might bring some milk and butter too."

"What time do you think the ceremony will start? I don't want to miss any of it."

"Oh, they'll get going about midnight. You got lots of time."

"Midnight! I heard that it was to start about now."

"Who told you that? It always starts late and goes on all night. Come back and have some mutton stew and frybread with us. We're going to watch TV until they're ready."

My round trip to the store took almost an hour and a half. I returned about eight-thirty and took the food into the mobile home. Lucy took a Diet Pepsi to Mary, and a regular Pepsi to the medicine man. Then she served me a plate of mutton stew with a big piece of frybread and hot coffee. The TV, hooked up to a large satellite dish in the yard, blared a basketball game under way in Kentucky. Country-western music roared from a radio in the kitchen. A warm fire crackled in the cast-iron stove, the only source of heat in the home.

The whole scene fascinated me. Here I was, in the middle of the Navajo Reservation, eating frybread and mutton stew, watching a ball game being played more than a thousand miles away. Only a few yards from where I sat, a medicine man, who spoke no English, was in meditation about an ancient ritual he would soon perform for Mary Begay. Bright young Navajo children played with toys and games. Relatives drifted in and out, and the table-talk, switching from English to Navajo and back again, was warm and cheerful. Everyone wanted to know about me. I was certainly no stranger to the family, but I was to be the only *belagáana*, or white man, at the ceremony.

At eleven-thirty, one of the daughters remarked, "Well, it's getting about time. I think that we should see if Mom and the medicine man want something to eat. They've been resting all evening."

She disappeared out the door of the trailer house and headed for the hogan. Having consumed quarts of coffee, I needed to use the bathroom. Once the ceremony started I'd be unable to leave.

John, Mary's son, laughed when I asked about the bathroom. "Oh, we never got the water hooked up. Look at all that stuff in the kitchen. We never even been able to use the dishwasher. The bathroom is down the hall, but there's no water. We still have to carry all the water from town until we get money for the well driller. The john is up the hill, or if you get far enough from the house, go behind a tree."

I wondered about priorities. Personally, I'd rather have a working bathroom than a satellite dish, but this was not my home.

I walked into the cold November night. A strong wind intensified the cold. But something bothered me more than the wind, the cold, and the darkness. I had the feeling that creatures, beings of some sort, lurked nearby. A chill ran up my back. All the stories of skinwalkers and witches came to mind. Those creatures of the night are said to live near this place. Indeed, we had talked around the table about skinwalkers and witches. Mary, herself, had been witched several times. Other Navajo families living near Mary Begay had been witched. People talked openly about it.

I knew, without doubt, that a skinwalker was out there near where I was trying to relieve myself. My imagination ran rampant. I began shaking uncontrollably as the night chill and the lurking evil honed my anxiety. I felt a presence, something practically touching me. I walked awkwardly, half zipped, back to the well-lit safety of the mobile home. In the light the threat seemed less real.

"Come on, Jackson," Lucy said. "We gotta go to the hogan now and clean up the dishes. The medicine man is ready. By the way, did you see any skinwalkers out there? I don't like to go out there at night, but later they will all be gone—all the ghosts, spirits, skinwalkers, and witches. Mr. Yellowhair is going to get rid of them."

I was still shivering when we entered the hogan. I looked at Mary and noted her fatigue. She was a lovely woman, in her late 40s or early 50s, but that night she looked much older. We carried the dishes back to the trailer house, picked up some soft drinks, and returned to the hogan. I walked a little faster than normal as we passed by the spot where I thought someone had been watching. But there was no sound except the TV and the wind whistling through the piñons.

Back at the hogan many of the friends and relatives had already taken their seats on the dirt floor. Blankets and pillows served as cushions against the wall. The only door opened toward the east. I nodded a greeting to all who looked directly at me. I knew many of the twenty or more people present. Most were Mary's family: children, sisters, nieces, nephews. Several older ladies eyed me with suspicion. I suppose my white skin and bald head stood out in sharp contrast to the reddish-brown skin tones of the Navajo. Mary sat on the floor against the west wall of the hogan with Mr. Yellowhair on her right. She looked calm but pale. Yellowhair, busy arranging his medicines, herbs, and fetishes, didn't give me a glance. Fire blazed furiously in a sheetmetal stove at the center of the octagonal hogan. The overheated stovepipe glowed red-orange. I thought briefly about the fire danger from this stove, but the heat felt good. At last I stopped shivering and I began to absorb the drama of the ceremony about to take place.

John motioned for me to sit along the south wall next to him. I started toward him, passing directly in front of the stove. He waved me away saying, "No! Not that way! Always walk clockwise and then circle the stove in front of Mom and the medicine man. Then you can come here to take your seat."

Yellowhair continued to inspect and arrange his medicines and potions. Finally, apparently satisfied, he washed his hands and at the same time started to cough; a bone-rattling, nerve-shattering cough. He doubled up in pain, and his face turned almost black. Tears rolled down his face, and his body shook as he struggled to get his breath. I wondered if he might have tuberculosis or lung cancer. Finally, he controlled the cough, wiped his eyes, and leaned forward. He began to arrange and inspect the items he had taken from the medicine bag. Then he stood for a moment, walked up to the stove, squatted to inspect the fire, and returned to his seat next to Mary. He wore a dark red bandana, blue jeans, a brightly colored western shirt, and handmade leather moccasins. A long string of old turquoise nuggets hung from his neck and there were several old silver bracelets on his arms. A thin, dry old man with a heavily lined face and dark eyes, he commanded respect.

I didn't know what would be expected of me during the ceremony. Was I to be merely a casual observer, a silent witness, or would I participate along with the others in the hogan?

I looked at John. He whispered, "Jackson, you sit right here next to Ellis, my cousin, and we'll tell you what to do. The medicine man is going to pass around some rattles. You take one and hold it. When Yellowhair shakes his rattle and Ellis rattles his, you rattle yours. Keep it in time with the medicine man and Ellis. Don't be afraid of rattling it as hard as you can." He smiled and whispered, "You're gonna do a lotta rattlin', tonight."

I asked what else I might do. "I want to make a few notes as we go along. Is that okay? I don't want to do anything that will disturb your mom's healing."

"Yeah, it's okay. Just scribble so you can remember. You don't have a tape recorder, do you?"

I assured him that I didn't. Ellis handed me a rattle made from dry, hard leather, trimmed with eagle or hawk feathers. I looked at it carefully and noted that a constellation of stars, which I couldn't identify, was etched on its smooth surface. I waited for the ceremony to start, feeling self-conscious. It seemed that all eyes were on me. Ellie Watson, Mary's sister, entered the hogan and nodded at me. I smiled at her and looked around the dimly lit hogan for more familiar faces. The rattle felt good in my hand. My small note pad rested on my knee. I was warm and secure.

John left the hogan and returned with a small can and a piece of brown wrapping paper. He knelt on the floor in front of Yellowhair, took some charcoal from the can, placed it on the paper, and wrapped it up. Twisting and mashing, he broke up the charcoal, then he rolled the tin can back and forth over the brown paper to reduce the charcoal to a black powder.

Yellowhair began to chant, and Ellis began to rattle gently. I followed Ellis. John placed the paper and charcoal near Mary and Yellowhair. Next he took ashes from the stove and placed them in small piles on each side of the stove. Then he took another small scoop of ashes from the stove to the door of the hogan. He opened it and brushed aside the blanket that had been hung to cover the cracks in the door. Cold poured through the open doorway as he scattered the ashes directly outside.

Yellowhair increased the cadence of the chant. Ellis and I followed suit, and Yellowhair slipped into a semitrance. He squatted on his haunches with one ear cupped in his right hand, almost as if he were listening for a distant command. His left hand worked a rattle. His voice had a hypnotic quality. Mary sat with closed eyes.

Suddenly, without signal, Mary stood and walked around the fire in a clockwise direction. She returned to her seat and began to remove her necklace, then her belt, and her blouse and brassiere. She sat with eyes half-closed.

The chanting continued. John walked to the door with a bull-roarer in his hand. A bull-roarer is a primitive tool attached to a long leather cord. When swung overhead it emits a roaring, moaning sound that may be changed by increasing or decreasing the speed with which it is whirled.

The door closed behind John, but we still heard the mournful whine of the bull-roarer. He was not gone long, perhaps a minute or so, then he returned to the hogan and touched the bull-roarer to Mary's feet, her bare breasts, her head, and bare back. Careful of the object's power, John handled it gently. After he had rolled the cord around the roarer he placed it next to Yellowhair and took his seat beside me.

"Do you know what this is all about, Jackson?" he asked.

"No," I replied, "I have no idea except that it's a healing ceremony."

Mary had been the victim of several witchcraft incidents in the years I had known her. Many Navajo neighbors, even relatives, were jealous of her weaving ability and her income from the

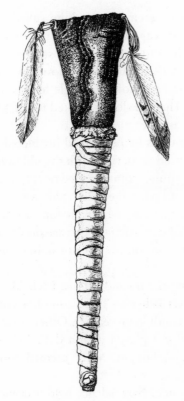

*"You're gonna do a lotta rattlin'
tonight."*

weaving. I saw several women in the room whom family members
suspected of being involved in witchcraft.

John explained, "A long time ago, maybe twenty years or more,
Mom gave birth to twins who were born dead. She never saw them.
The hospital never told her where they were buried. Now, after all
this time, and after all her sickness, a handtrembler told her the
spirits of these two children were haunting her body. The bodies
should have been placed in the limb of a north-facing dead tree and
allowed to rest there. Instead, someone buried them someplace.
They didn't return to the spirit world. They are confused and they
keep returning to haunt my mother. This ceremony confuses them.
We will change her appearance so they will not recognize her and
will leave her alone."

I thought it might be a Ghostway ceremony, but John called it a Deathway or Evilway. Whatever it was called, it was happening. Yellowhair's chants continued, the rattles rattled. Most of those present closed their eyes to meditate, intent on the power we all sensed. Yellowhair rose to his feet and took two eagle-feather fetishes from his medicine bundle. Then he slowly walked to the fire and dipped the feathers in ashes and began to bless the room. He turned to all sides facing each of us as he performed his blessing, still chanting softly. Ellis and I rattled on in time with the old man.

During a lull in the ceremony a young woman seated next to Ellis whispered she could not understand what the Yellowhair was saying. "He speaks Navajo words I have never heard before. I think that this must be an old, old part of our language that we don't use anymore. It's spooky to recognize the sounds but not understand the words."

Caught up in the rhythm of the chants and rattles, I felt like a puppet on a long string, guided yet believing I had complete control. I floated weightlessly like a windblown feather. Others in the hogan swayed in unison. A small girl played with a doll. An old lady sat with closed eyes, deep in thought. Mary seemed completely in Yellowhair's power.

Yellowhair returned to Mary's side. Now silence held everyone as the aged medicine man infused a bowl of water with herbs from several small paper bags. A subtle, yet pungent aroma drifted around us. Suddenly, without command, John sprang up from his seat and approached the medicine man. He took the bowl from Yellowhair, dipped his right hand into the mixture, and began rubbing it on his own forehead, then he sipped from the bowl. He held a mouthful for a few moments before walking clockwise around the fire to where I was seated. As he held the bowl in front of me I asked in a bewildered whisper, "What am I supposed to do?"

"Just take a little bit, hold it in your mouth, and taste it. Then take some of the stuff out of your mouth and rub it on your head, your chest, and any place you need healing."

The potion tasted like a mixture of sagebrush, juniper, piñon, and chamisa—a blend of bitter and sweet. I held it in my mouth for a few seconds, as John moved on to Ellis. I then took most of the pulp from my mouth and used my fingers to rub it on my forehead and chest. I had recently been treated for prostate cancer, so I gently rubbed a small amount on my pants near my crotch. I looked up in time to see one of Mary's daughters smile and nudge her sister with her elbow. I smiled back.

Ellis and the others who followed him placed their hands into the bowl and took whole gobs of the pulp out and put it in their mouths. I was glad that I'd been first. After Ellis and the young man next to him had served themselves, they began to snicker and joke with each other about Yellowhair. They wouldn't laugh in his face, but like the rest of us, they needed a little levity. I was reminded of two irreverent altar boys making faces behind a priest's back during Mass.

When everyone, including Mary, had tasted the brew, John put his fingers into it and began to flick it around the interior of the hogan in all directions. The medicine man resumed a soft chant, which continued until John had taken the remainder of the potion outside the hogan and disposed of it. I assume he tossed it to the winds. Mary sat quietly, stripped to the waist with her long hair hanging loosely. It streamed down her back almost touching the ground. Her eyes closed in meditation, her head bowed forward, she was a beautiful woman despite her illness. I thought about the times in the past few months that I had come by to watch her weave. Two years earlier Toh-Atin Gallery in Durango had advanced Mary several thousand dollars as partial payment for the rug now on her loom. We now had a big stake in its completion. If anything were to happen to Mary, no other person would be able to finish the weaving.

John returned to Mary's side. He opened a jar of oil and she dipped her fingers into it. Slowly, she rubbed the oil on her breasts, stomach, and face. John applied it to her back. The oil made her skin glisten as the dim light played on her body. Mary lifted her long skirts above her knees and rubbed oil on her legs. After her body and face had been thoroughly covered with oil, John opened the paper that held the powdered charcoal. Together he and Mary rubbed the charcoal on her oiled, shining skin.

The charcoal stuck to the oil and her skin changed texture as the oil absorbed the jet black powder. John made sure he covered every part of her upper body. Mary lifted her skirts and rubbed the dull black powder over her lower and upper legs, front and back, until she was covered from her toes to her crotch, fully disguised.

Yellowhair continued chanting, but suddenly the chant had a new rhythm and sound. My rattle kept pace with his voice, which rose and fell in hypnotic pulse. All eyes were on Mary and John; this was a crucial point. John worked rapidly, as if on a deadline. I marveled at his soft touch, his love and respect for his mother, and, above all, his knowledge of the ceremony. I had known him in the past as a jovial, rather carefree young family man with a good job in Window Rock and a taste for country-western music. This was an entirely different fellow.

Finally satisfied that Mary's body was completely covered, John began to apply a white clay paste in silver-dollar-size spots. I lost count, but there must have been over a hundred white spots on her body. John knelt in front of Mary, looking directly into her eyes for a few moments, as if to say, "You look different. I hardly recognize you."

Then, to complete the transformation in her appearance, he began to paint her face with red ochre paint, accenting the tilt of her eyes and changing the shape of her mouth. John gathered her hair on top of her head and placed feathered fetishes and arrowheads in it. I couldn't take my eyes off her. John then dabbed the red ochre on his own face, emphasizing his eyes and mouth to fierce effect.

Yellowhair's chanting grew louder, and the tempo of the song increased. His voice ranged from low guttural tones to a high-pitched wail. I continued to rattle. Everyone in the hogan stared at Mary's transformation. John gave Mary two long strings of turquoise beads. She placed one string over her left shoulder and under her right arm, and one over the right shoulder and under the left arm, bandolier fashion. He tied a pure white ribbon around her neck and gave her all her fine turquoise and silver jewelry, which she placed around her neck and on her wrists. Then she reached down to put on her shoes and sat back to relax.

Without warning or command the chanting and rattling stopped. I continued to rattle for several beats, and one of the young girls snickered and winked at me. Yellowhair stood up, stretched, and walked about the hogan. John came back to sit beside me.

"We're gonna have a break. I think that this is even too heavy for Yellowhair. If you want to go outside for a moment, it's okay."

I remembered my fear earlier by the trees and decided I could wait. The fire felt good and I was with people.

Yellowhair began to tell a story in Navajo. John interpreted for me. "He says that one time he was in the middle of a ceremony like this for a man who lived near Tuba City. The patient got real upset and walked out of the hogan. Yellowhair had to run out and bring him back, and they had to start the ceremony all over again. Then the patient ran out again and Yellowhair brought him back for a second time."

All the Navajos in the hogan laughed. Mary giggled. Even Yellowhair smiled. Suddenly, he turned and looked toward me and began to speak. Everyone got real quiet. I thought that maybe he was going to take my meager notes and send me out into the dark to be at the mercy of the night creatures. Everyone looked at me. John leaned over, smiled, and whispered, "He says he is glad that you are here."

Almost immediately the medicine man returned to his seat and began to chant again. At one point he stopped and began to cough again for a few moments. Everyone watched as he struggled to gain his breath. Though he was obviously afflicted with a severe lung problem, no one in the hogan seemed concerned. I looked around the hogan and smiled as I saw John and his two young male friends chewing tobacco and spitting into an empty pop can.

The short recess had broken the tension. Later I realized that it had been deliberate. The charcoal, the white clay dots, and the elaborate paint had been planned to confuse the evil spirits. A change of mood enhanced the deception. Yellowhair began to chant again, and the rattles once more began to rattle. Proud of myself, I thought, "I'm getting quite good at this. Maybe I can hire out as a ceremonial rattler."

John approached the fire again and added another piece of wood. It roared back to life, the stovepipe turned red and again thoughts of a hogan fire raced through my mind. John picked up the bull-roarer and walked outside, a blast of cold air rushing in as he exited. Soon I heard the voice of the bull-roarer, a full-blown, spine-tingling roar, as

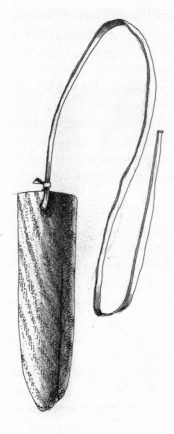

Bull roarer.

John beckoned the spirits of the dead babies. Time and time again he summoned them.

After five or ten minutes he reentered the hogan, walked clockwise around the fire, and placed the roarer against Mary's head, back, bare breasts, and feet. She sat with eyes wide open, grotesque in her altered appearance. She removed her shoes and John rubbed the contraption against each foot. He took the roarer outside again and worked it for another minute or so before coming in and resuming his seat. Almost immediately he rose in seeming afterthought, went to Mary who was still shirtless, and placed a blanket over her shoulders. Despite the roaring fire, a chill had descended in the hogan. It was almost 3:00 A.M.

John came over to sit beside me. "We painted all that stuff on Mom so that the spirit of those dead twins would not recognize her. I had to make sure, and I went out and called them to come. That's what the roarer is for. I tried twice, and they didn't come. She is changed, and the spirits are confused and have gone away. They won't bother her anymore, but she has to wear that paint and charcoal for a few days just to make sure."

He continued, "The medicine man says he is going to sing that last chant five more times. Each chant takes about five minutes, so in about thirty minutes it will all be over. We are going to stay here until the sun comes up. But the healing part is all over, and you can leave if you want to after the prayer and the chant."

Mary looked exhausted, even through the heavy paint on her face. The heat in the hogan and the hypnotic chanting had taken their toll. An older man slept in fetal position, head in his wife's lap. His snores added a touch of reality to what had been a most unreal evening. Yellowhair chanted five more times, and I rattled the rattle. I was relieved that it was almost over, but I wondered if I would ever have another chance to see a ceremony like this.

When the chanting was over, Yellowhair said a long prayer. John said that he thanked the animals for being friends to the Navajo, thanked the deities for their blessing and for the bounty the people enjoyed in their daily life. He said that the land and the water and the sky did not belong to us, but belonged to Mother Nature, and that we were only borrowing it. Then he turned to me and spoke. He didn't smile and his voice showed little emotion. He talked for what seemed like ten minutes. John listened intently, then interpreted.

"Mr. Yellowhair says that he thanks you for all that you and your family have done for Mary and her family. He wishes that you have a safe journey and a long life and happiness."

John said there would be a short break and offered me a cup of coffee. I declined. Somehow coffee seemed anticlimactic.

"Jackson, you can leave now, if you like. Just get up and walk clockwise around the room and shake hands with everyone. Be sure to shake hands and thank Yellowhair. All of us are glad that you could come."

I shook everyone's hand and stepped into the clear, cold, pre-dawn air. The stars were out, and the waning moon was directly overhead. I walked to the spot where I had gone to relieve myself before the ceremony. The temperature was at least twenty degrees colder, but the early morning seemed less threatening. The cedar and piñon rustled softly. Whatever evil that had been there earlier was gone. I walked to my car in peace and beauty, full of thanksgiving, and drove the forty miles to Chinle with only my thoughts for company.

Mary's health improved, and she resumed weaving the large rug. When I next visited her, she looked well and said so. Navajo medicine and Mr. Yellowhair had given her peace of mind and strength of body. The ghosts of the dead twins did not return to the Begay home.

The Medicine Man and the Preacher

Juan Begay, Navajo medicine man, met Paul Benally, Navajo evangelist, at Toh-Atin in Durango one day in 1982. It was a collision of personalities, beliefs, and willpower. I can look back on it now and laugh. But at the time it wasn't funny.

I was talking to Juan and his daughter Virgie at the time, when Paul Benally's daughter, Josie, unexpectedly poked her head into the rug display room. Josie is an expert weaver. Juan Begay and I were on our knees carefully examining a Navajo medicine-man's bundle I had acquired several years before from a trading post on the reservation. I didn't hear the door open and I was startled when Josie spoke.

"Hello, Mr. Clark. I brought that rug I was telling you about." Her eyes were on Juan and Virgie Begay. "Do you want to see it? I have to sell it today 'cause I need some money *real bad*."

Still kneeling, I said, "Sure I want to see it. I didn't know you were driving up today. I'm real busy right now. Can you wait in the entry hall? I'll be out in a few minutes."

I wanted to see her rug, but at that moment I had the medicine bundle on my mind. I had waited a long time for someone to tell me about it, and Juan Begay had come along at the right time. Josie Benally could wait a few minutes.

Speaking in Navajo as his daughter translated, Begay said that it was a most unusual bundle. It had probably been used in the

Nightway chant and other winter ceremonies and was very old. Filled with wonderful objects like rattles, beads, wands, fetishes, and sketches of sand paintings, it intrigued Begay. I knew little about medicine bundles, sand painters' kits, and the like, but I knew I had something special — something culturally significant.

Virgie said, "My father says there's a lot of power in these things. He wants to know if you will sell it to him; it should be used by a Navajo medicine man and not given to a museum or sold to a white person."

I had planned to donate the bundle to the University of Colorado Museum for their permanent collection. However, if an honest-to-goodness medicine man could actually use it for healing, I might reconsider. I liked Juan Begay although he never looked me in the eye. He avoided eye contact and seemed ill at ease when I questioned him. Virgie sensed this.

"My father doesn't deal much with traders. He only works with the Navajo people who need his help. He's shy because he can't speak good English. He understands everything we say, but he doesn't want to speak."

Juan Begay nodded. I watched him as he caressed each item in the kit. I had known Virgie for about a year. She and her sister were occasional weavers and full-time students at Fort Lewis College. They wove high-quality pillow coverings and small rugs. Their mother made miniature Navajo looms.

We continued examining the kit for thirty minutes or so before I suddenly remembered Josie Benally and her rug. I needed a break to give me time to consider Juan Begay's offer. I expected whatever we worked out would be strictly barter — just rugs, looms, maybe jewelry in trade for the medicine bundle. We had talked about price. I took an eyeball inventory of the kit and asked the Begays to wait for me.

Josie was waiting in the hall. She said, "You remember my father, Reverend Benally, don't you, Mr. Clark? He's an evangelist and he lives near Tuba City. He wanted to ride in with me because he has some business to do here."

I did remember her father. He was a short, stocky Navajo with a game leg. He had a droopy eyelid that fluttered closed and open like a camera shutter. I judged him to be eight or ten years older than myself.

Medicine bundle.

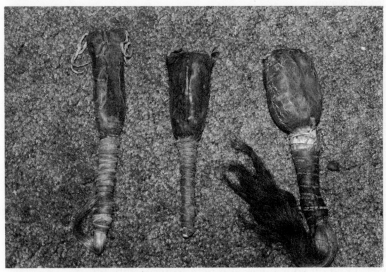

"It was filled with wonderful things. . . ."

I asked if they could wait just a few minutes more, but before they could answer Virgie Begay stepped into the hallway. She looked startled and immediately turned on her heels and fled back into the rug room, leaving the door open. I saw Juan Begay, still on his knees examining the medicine bundle. The Reverend Mr. Benally saw him too. He wheeled around on his bad leg, almost falling to the floor, and shouted at me in English, "What's that man doing in there on his knees? Is he praying to Jesus or the devil? Do you know him? He's an evil Navajo. He hurts people. Why do you have him here?"

To say I was shocked is an understatement. I was stunned. Then I got mad.

"He's a friend of mine. He's here with his daughter just like you are. What the hell's the matter with you?"

Josie Benally backed into the corner of the hallway, clutching her still unseen weaving close to her breast, and covering her eyes with her hands. She shook violently as she listened to her father speaking in Navajo.

She stammered, "My father says that this man is evil."

Juan Begay calmly contemplated a fetish from the bundle. He didn't look at Benally. Virgie Begay had fled the rug room through my office. The Reverend Mr. Benally shouted at the top of his lungs about the "evil man." Josie cowered in the corner. Medicine Man Begay never blinked.

Suddenly, Benally grabbed my hand and led me through the rug room door. He lurched and limped by the kneeling Juan Begay, still shouting about Jesus, the devil, evil. . . .

In my office, he slammed the door and slowly dropped to his knees. He raised his hands over his head and closed his eyes. "You're a veteran, aren't you, Mr. Clark? Didn't you fight the Germans?" He gave me no time to answer. "The Germans were evil but you don't know what evil is. Drop to your knees, Mr. Clark. Get down on your knees and pray to Jesus with me."

Still in a state of shock I thought the best way to handle the situation was to do what he said and hope that it would be over quickly. Benally shrieked his prayer in a high-pitched, rasping voice. "Oh Mighty Lord, protect Mr. Clark from this evil man.

Protect Mr. Clark, a fellow veteran who fought evil in Germany. Guide him away from the power of the man in the next room."

He held my wrist in a vise-like grip. Beads of sweat ran down his face, and his whole body trembled. His bad eye opened and closed like a flashing light. The whole scene was unreal. Then suddenly there was only silence for what seemed like minutes. The preacher slowly lowered his arms and rose unsteadily to his feet. I wondered if he had been drinking or was on some drug.

By this time the racket had alarmed everyone in the Pepsi office in the next room. Several people rushed into the room to see what was happening. I assured them that it was okay, but now I was really irritated with the good Reverend. I thought it was all over, but Benally roared on. "Protect Mr. Clark, his family, and his employees from this evil man and his witchcraft. I beseech you, Lord. Hear my prayer. Amen."

Witchcraft! Had he said witchcraft? It kept getting more weird with each passing moment. Suddenly Benally pitched forward, almost falling to the floor. I helped him steady himself and let him catch his breath.

"I don't know what to say to you, Reverend Benally. I appreciate your concern, but you butted into my business. I'd appreciate it if you would keep your voice down so that everyone doesn't hear us. Okay? Now tell me about this witchcraft business. You're a Christian? And you're not supposed to believe in witches."

Gasping for air and pointing toward the next room, he screamed, "I know only one witch. That man in the other room is the one. I don't want to talk about witchcraft, but that man is evil. Don't let him have the medicine bundle. Burn it or give it away, but don't give it to him. He will destroy you. I must leave. This place has a bad feeling."

With that he limped from my office into the rug room. Juan Begay and Virgie were gone. The medicine bundle was where Juan had left it. All the items had been neatly arranged in rows. It was over as suddenly as it began. The Reverend Mr. Benally and Josie left the building. I never saw them again. Nor did I ever see Juan Begay again. Virgie told me he was working near Round Rock. Virgie, her sister, and her mother continued to come to Toh-Atin to sell rugs.

Virgie and I never talked about the medicine bundle and the Benally incident. The medicine bundle is in the University of Colorado Museum for scholars to study. I often wonder what might have happened if Juan Begay had bought it from me. Would it have been used in healing or used for other purposes? Was he as evil as Benally believed, or was he merely the object of an old man's rage? I'll never know.

The Owl in Monument Canyon

Owls, creatures of the night, play a prominent role in Navajo mythology, ceremonies, and witchcraft. Navajo families will often delay a trip if an owl is seen hanging around near their hogan.

"We didn't leave today because that owl was in the tree all night long. (*It's always* that *owl.*) We can't leave as long as he's hangin' around." So said John Harvey about failing to show up at my house in Chinle, Arizona, at an appointed time. Some Navajos say that humans can transform themselves into owls to scout their enemies. Some Indian legends say that when an owl calls your name death is near.

It was a warm October day in 1987 when I hiked down into the depths of Monument Canyon, a remote branch of Canyon de Chelly, with Russ, a park ranger, Joel, a friend of mine from Durango, and Nan, my friend from Chinle. I couldn't imagine a more perfect day. The sky was a turquoise blue, the chamisa in full bloom, and wildflowers everywhere. Not a cloud in sight. We planned to walk until midafternoon and then work our way back up to arrive back at the car well before dark. We looked at the map and knew we had a long way to go—maybe five miles or more each way.

We followed the steep, rough trail down into the canyon. I kept thinking that we had to come back this way—hopefully before dark. Oh, well, what the hell. These guys know what they're doing.

189

Enjoy! Russ reassured us, "We'll get back here to the car before sundown. Let's travel light so we can make good time."

Traveling light meant taking only a canteen of water, a sandwich, an apple, cameras and binoculars, and sunscreen. I took the flashlight out of my daypack and left it in the car. No need for that thing. I'm terribly nearsighted, so just in case something happened to my dark glasses I took my clear, prescription glasses. We'd be back at the car by sundown.

It took an hour to reach the canyon floor. Then we headed for a group of ruins we had spotted on the map. They were several miles farther up the canyon. The sunshine, the bright blue sky, and the excitement of the quest made it easy to forget the time. Deep shadows began to fall in the canyon. It was 5:00 P.M.

We had found the ruins, eaten our lunch at the base of Spider Rock, and observed a colony of beavers happily chomping the cottonwoods on the banks of a small stream. It had been a perfect day, like most fall days in the Southwest. Time had slipped by. Russ said, "I think we'd better haul out of here. We may have to climb the steep part of the trail in the moonlight."

Joel laughed and said, "There's no moon tonight. We are in the dark of the moon, but we'll be okay."

Joel is a wiry little guy with incredible physical strength. He just doesn't know when to quit. That day he had scaled a cliff and scampered up steep slopes all day searching for an Anasazi ladder that might lead him to the ruin. After we found the ruin high above us in the cliff, I told him, "Hey, we found it. There it is. You don't have to go up there."

"I want to take some photos from up there so I can have the same view as the Anasazi."

We had watched as he clawed his way from ledge to ledge, camera banging into the wall. Several times he had to inch his way along a ledge after finding no way up or down. When we tried to shout directions to him our words were drowned by echos bouncing back from the cliffs. We decided it was better to just watch. I told Russ that I hoped that if Joel fell we'd be able to bury him right there—and tell his mother what happened. His climbing made me uneasy. When he finally scrambled down I was tired from just watching and walking the long trail. Joel seemed as fresh and eager as when we started.

Heading back we walked by a few Navajo hogans and two flocks of Navajo sheep guarded by watchful, silent dogs who kept themselves between us and the herd. We heard no sounds, saw no humans, and met few birds or squirrels but quickened our pace as shadows crept up the nine-hundred-foot canyon walls. The sky turned from turquoise to violet to indigo and then, finally, as we were halfway up the steep trail, all light was gone. The stars shone brightly. The Milky Way looked like a lace curtain under a skylight. Darkness had fallen almost instantly.

I stopped to change from my dark glasses into the clear lenses. I had the clear glasses out to put them on when they slipped from my hand. They fell to the rocks on the side of the trail, then bounced over the edge and down into the depths of the canyon. The sound of breaking glass echoed up the canyon. I never saw them. It was dark, and without them I was blind.

I tried the dark glasses. Then I tried no glasses at all. It was like being trapped in a coal mine, only worse. We were on a hazardous trail with steep drop-offs, unseen rock ledges in the trail itself, and occasional low-hanging branches from the piñon, pine, and oak-brush. I was helpless, nervous, and almost blind. The party was over, and we were a long way from anywhere.

The trail switchbacked up the wall of the canyon, reversing itself every fifty to sixty feet. Twice I stumbled and almost fell as I missed a sharp turn. Russ lost the trail twice and ran into the brush. We laughed and joked about the blind leading the blind, but it was really no laughing matter. We were at least an hour away from the canyon rim and unsure where we would come out.

Suddenly, Russ paused to catch his breath. "Quiet! Listen! Did you hear that?"

Joel had. I had. Then we heard it again. Then we could feel it. Movement above us. Just a rush of air—very faint rush of air and slightly ahead of us.

Joel whispered, "It's an owl."

It swooshed close enough to graze my hat and made another quick pass directly overhead. Then it landed. Unseen, it perched until we

were close and then it rushed above our heads again, landing somewhere else until we caught up.

Joel said, "I wonder if it's trying to lead us out of here. Let's be
quiet and follow it."

Follow it we did, slowly, steadily up the trail, around turns and
switchbacks as the owl pointed the way. Once we made the wrong
turn and it swooped low overhead pointing the way with sound until we found the trail again.

Helpless without my glasses, I could not be sure the owl was on
our side or not. Our pace picked up. We had to listen. The owl was
with us. I thought for a moment that it might lead us off of a cliff,
but because I couldn't trust myself I decided to trust the owl.

Then suddenly we topped out on the canyon rim, not fifty feet
from our car. With a final pass, the owl left, as swiftly as it had
appeared.

We were all so disoriented from the hike that once in the car it
took several minutes to get headed in the right direction back to
Chinle. The night was pitch black. We passed no hogans, no cars,
no horses, no cattle. Nothing, until we rounded a bend and saw a
graying old coyote in the middle of the rutted road. His eyes glowed
fiery red in the headlights. He moved slowly out of the way as we
approached.

Remembering Navajo beliefs in owls and coyotes I wondered. No,
it couldn't be. Things like that just don't happen. Owls don't guide
people along dangerous trails. Owls don't become coyotes. Owls are
owls and coyotes are coyotes. Except, maybe, in Navajoland.